MW01615887

HEALING WITH

Crystals & Gemstones

HEALING WITH

Crystals & Gemstones

Balance Your Chakras and Your Life

Daya Sarai Chocron

WEISER BOOKS
Boston, MA/York Beach, ME

I dedicate this book to
TARA
Goddess of Compassion
who is my guiding Light

First published in 2005 by
Red Wheel/Weiser, LLC
York Beach, ME
With offices at:
368 Congress Street
Boston, MA 02210

ISBN: 0-7394-6091-9

Printed in the United States of America

Cover design by Kathleen Wilson Fivel
"Woman holding crystal, mid-section" by Kelvin Murray/Getty Images

Contents

Introduction to the 2005 Edition

As Daya Sarai Chocron points out, children are mesmerised by crystals. As a child, I picked up every pretty stone I saw. I rubbed it, absorbed its energies, spoke to it in the depths of the night, and it in turn spoke to me. Stones gave me companionship, wisdom, and peace. They were my friends and one in particular, a battered piece of quartz I had found in my grandmother's workbox, went everywhere with me. In this way I came to value not only the bright, shiny treasures of gemstones, but to appreciate also the quieter beauty of semi-precious stones and the beneficial energies of outwardly unlovely crystals.

As someone with such a close connection to the mineral kingdom, I instinctively recognized in Daya Sarai Chocron a fellow crystal devotee and someone who was as passionately connected to her crystals as I am. And I was delighted to see that she had included in her book the healing properties of the quieter, but equally hardworking, opaque stones and not just the showy stars of the gem world.

Unlike many adults, I never lost my attraction to crystals, and it was my fascination for the stones and their healing powers that led me to write my own book on crystals called the *The Crystal Bible*.

Even as I write this introduction, I am surrounded by crystals. They energize and inform my life daily, just as they have for others through the centuries.

Admired for their decorative qualities, gemstones have graced kings, queens, and commoners alike throughout history. However, there is far more to crystals than simple beauty. For millennia these gifts from the earth have been used for healing and shamanic ceremonies. Although now regarded as "New Age," crystal wands, mirrors, balls, and other healing tools have been found in ancient British burial mounds, Egyptian tombs, and Mayan ruins. Evidence of their use has also been discovered in the Native American, Indian, Tibetan, and Chinese cultures, as well as the Australian Aboriginal and Siberian shamanic traditions. The wisdom from these ancient cultures has been carried forward as a body of hidden crystal lore that includes the use of birthstones, amulets, and talismans, as well as the ingredients of natural medicines. Stones have been pulverized and used as healing potions for centuries. Nowadays, crystals are worn or placed on the body to bring about health and well-being.

As more and more people are rediscovering, crystal healing is a highly effective method of harnessing the magical power of the natural world. Good health is a sensitive balance of various factors, many of which occur at a subtle, bioelectric or biomagnetic level. It is with these subtle fields that crystals interact to bring about healing. With their gentle, non-invasive energies, crystals and gemstones are the perfect way to promote holistic health. That is to say, crystals rebalance and harmonize physical, emotional, mental, and spiritual energies within the body and the biomagnetic sheath that surrounds it. Having no side effects, crystals cannot cause harm or create life-denying addictions, and they are easy to apply once you know how. There are no complicated procedures or special equipment needed for crystal healing. Many times a crystal in your pocket and the time to relax and enjoy its benefits are all that is necessary.

Crystal healing does not work primarily with symptoms. It is more concerned with overall health and well-being and with psychosomatic factors such as emotion and attitude and the effects of stress. Crystals can gently change destructive attitudes, create emotional stability, and provide support during the more challenging moments of life. They can also alleviate pain, protect and enhance your home and your environment, and improve your relationships. An excellent aid to meditation, they boost energies and calm the mind, taking you into another world.

With such a wide choice of crystals and a plethora of healing methods and theories now available, it is important to understand how and why crystals work and to connect to their esoteric properties. It is also helpful to have a deep grounding in the metaphysical laws that underlie the processes of health and dis-ease. This is why *Healing with Crystals and Gemstones* is such a useful addition to your crystal library.

In her enlightening and inspiring work, Daya Sarai Chocron takes us deep into the hidden properties of crystals, the chakra system, and the subtle energies that underlie good health. Her loving connection with the natural world—and with her crystal allies—shines out from every page. The book is essentially practical and easy to use, based as it is on color and correspondences. Underlying its clarity and simplicity is a profound knowledge of what the stones do and the natural laws that govern their use. This awareness clearly arises from Chocron's years of working shamanically with her crystal friends. She is in spiritual and energetic communion with them, knows their properties intimately, and has the wisdom and intuition to apply them effectively.

This book is a course in esoteric crystal healing. The section on using the stones in relation to the chakras is particularly useful, clarifying as it does the links between the physical and spiritual effects of placing the stones on the chakras, and it is refreshing to find a crystal-healing book that places an equal emphasis on the physical and spiritual sides of the healing.

As an astrologer myself, I particularly enjoyed Chocron's concise and yet deeply insightful links between crystals and the zodiac signs, but all her work is profound. If you follow her color system and the helpful pictorial layouts and crystal placings, you too will be able to avail yourself of her healing wisdom and bring balance and harmony to you, your family, and your friends. I have been studying and working intuitively with crystals all my life, and I was still able to learn much from this book.

Judy Hall
Author of *The Crystal Bible: A Definitive Guide to Crystals*,
The Art of Psychic Protection and *The Hades Moon*

Introduction

I stand full of awe and wonder when I consider the beauty and abundance of our Mother Earth. It is through this love that we meet at this time.

Many years ago, after living on an island, I came back to the United States and started to learn about holistic health. At the time I also became interested in the American Indian way, for it seemed to be in tune with mother earth, the elements, the sacred. I spent several years in the Southwest—Colorado, New Mexico, and Arizona—learning new ways of healing, which were actually ancient ways, and eventually experienced a spiritual awakening.

Several teachers came: in Arizona, after spending a lot of time visiting and living on Indian reservations, I moved to the mountains. I would take long walks, feeling the power of the stones and rocks there. I believed that the rocks were guardians with many message for me, if I could but hear them. While there, I met a man, a lapidary, who was also very influenced by the sacredness of the Indian way. He was deep in communion with the crystals and stones. He shared much of the knowledge he channelled about their unique properties with me. Once he organized a meditation in a mine—deep in the earth. That experience changed my life. I truly felt the incredible power of the earth in that mine. We climbed down on rope ladders, lit candles, and in the dark deep earth, we chanted, prayed, thanked, and became one. He gave me the crystal that is now my faithful companion, going with me to workshops and healing sessions, and everywhere I travel.

A spark had been lit within me, and I went on to learn more with the Indian medicine women. They spoke of our connection with the animal, plant, and mineral kingdoms, of our union with the elements, of rituals and ceremonies with crystals and stones. They told of the stones' healing and spiritual qualities, of a way of living in harmony with the cosmos. They talked of the power and strength that is given to us from the mountains, the sea, the sun, the moon, the wind, the rain, the trees. One shamaness explained the importance of walking softly upon the earth so as not to disturb other kingdoms. Another spoke about the centering of the self through drumming, of the chant (or song) each one of us has been born to sing—and how we should find that song inside and give it to the world. I respect these teachings, and have tried to apply them in my daily life, and also want to pass them on.

Later I met a woman—a healer who was deeply involved with East Indian ways. An ancient sister had reappeared, and with her much exploration and experimentation happened. I learned about body massage, yogic meditation, the healing essence of flowers. We went into the desert to pick wild flowers to take home to make our own remedies. I became fascinated with the magical qualities of color. It is in flowers and stones that color is most perfectly manifested. They are soulmates to each other. I began working with color therapy, using visualization, meditation, and color candles. While working in a drug rehabilitation center—one that believed in using food as medicine and yoga to create changes in consciousness—I witnessed the powerful effects of these methods. This, too, I incorporated in my life. This remarkable woman, through her help and guidance, taught me counseling and demonstrated the art of selfless giving.

This mandala of various healing methods and various forms of training finally focused itself on healing with crystals and stones. Form is important to me, and a realization came that the crystals and stones, which are manifested forms of light and color, were to become my work, my purpose, my joy. I can touch and feel this earthly material filled with the spirit of light. The beauty of the stones touches my heart and nourishes my soul.

Love, which is an opening of the heart, is an act of faith—faith in potentiality. Loving requires courage, the ability to take a risk, the readiness to even accept pain and disappointment, and the willingness to grow. It is toward the goal of higher understanding and the opening of the hearts of humanity that my work is dedicated.

It takes time to learn to work with the crystals and stones. Although I studied many other facets of the healing experience, I prefer working with the stones. However, my other experience comes into play when I work with the stones, and I suggest that readers learn as much as they can in addition to the work with the stones. Much of my knowledge of the crystals and stones comes from an intuitional level, as many years of practice lets the stones "talk" to you. The stones pick me. They speak and I listen. This can only happen when you let yourself believe in the higher forces.

When working with the stones, I follow the laws of the chakras (which will be discussed in chapters 6 and 7) and you can use this information as a guide until you develop your own way. There are certain basic laws in the universe that are to be utilized, recognized and respected. Don't discard them—work with them lovingly! Also keep in mind that you become a channel for the stones when you work with them. You do not heal—the spirit in the stones heals. And the people you work with in the healing process actually heal themselves. Each person you work with is responsible for himself or herself; you can never become responsible for anyone but yourself. However, keep in mind that you should work with the stones in a responsible way.

I travel a great deal doing lectures, workshops and attending to a private treatment practice. The powerful effects and reactions that I have witnessed over the years reinforce my trust and confidence in the stones. I feel blessed in having been given this mission, and I hope this book will open a beautiful new world for you!

A Tibetan Buddhist proverb states, "If, after having been born a human being, One gives no heed to the Holy Doctrine, One resembleth a man who returneth empty-handed from a land rich in precious gems; and that is a grievous failure." This book came from a need to unburden myself, to reveal, and most of all, to perpetuate, this ancient tradition of healing and transformation through the aid of the stones—an organic way—from the earth.

La Roche St. Secret
Provence, France
Summer 1983

HEALING WITH

Crystals & Gemstones

1 Light and Color

LIGHT

One Universal Soul permeating all things,
which in substance resembles light.

Pythagoras

In our universe all light is an emanation from the central
Sun. The Sun is the storehouse of all energies and potencies,
the source of light, warmth, and motion on this planet.

Light is radiant energy. The visible universe manifests
on the physical plane through the cosmic forces of light,
form and vibration.

Ancient wisdom teaches that the universe evolved from
the primal cosmic fire or great white light, which is an
emanation of the Divine Being, the source of all light. The
Bhagavad Gita speaks of the imperishable light, "Behold the
Form of me in various kinds, in various colors." God,
according to the Hindu sages, is the "Shining One."

Light is the first syllable of the creative word, rhythmic
motion is the second, and color is the third. All radiations,
emitted from a luminous body, travel through space in
perfect rhythmic vibration in the form of waves or pulses.
The point of distance from crest to crest of these vibra-

tionary waves is called their wavelength, and their rate of vibration is called their frequency.

COLOR

The whole planet, the oceans, the earth, everything we see manifested as mineral, plant, animal and human, depends upon light and its amazing properties and radiations for its very existence. The etheric, astral, mental and spiritual planes depend upon this same source of light as well, for they each have their own rate of vibration.

Aside from aesthetic pleasure and beauty, color contributes more than any other factor (in a deep and subtle manner) to the transformation of spirit and soul. It is for this reason that tantric meditations give such importance to color. Color is a force of immeasurable and infinite power. It exerts a tremendous influence on the mind and emotions. It is the living language of light, the hallmark of conscious reality. Aldous Huxley came to the conclusion that color is the very touchstone of reality.

The science of color rests on the laws of light as manifested in the seven major rays. The color rays are related to the seven planets of manifestation, and the seven chakras (or wheels of light). Color is a mode of differentiation of the primal light according to its rate of vibration. The rates of vibration in colors vary a great deal—for example, violet light consists of very short waves, red light of much longer ones.

The highest vibration of all, the white light, is not generated by any individual—it is projected or transmitted to the aura from the cosmic source. The white light, or spiritual sun, enters the consciousness of the soul through the aura and is diffused into seven component colors. Each color infuses the appropriate soul center (or chakra) with power and vitality. (The word "soul" comes from sol or sun, which is the light center within our being.) Color expresses the very soul of the universe.

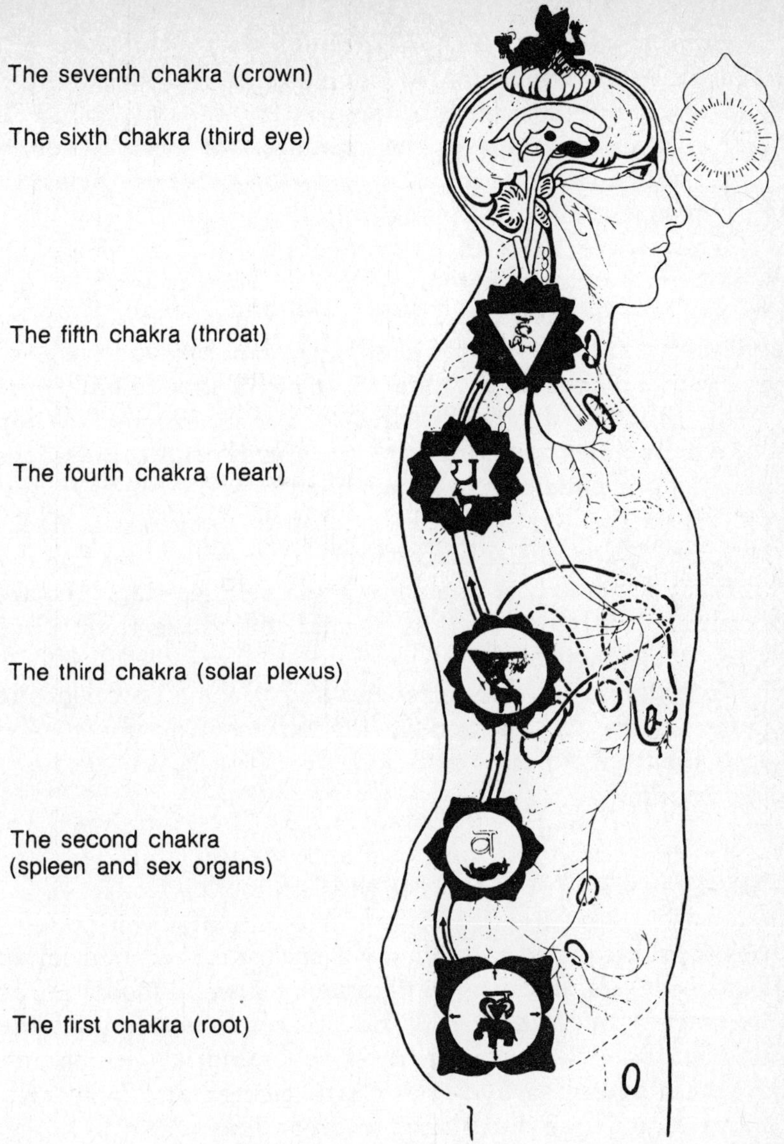

The seventh chakra (crown)

The sixth chakra (third eye)

The fifth chakra (throat)

The fourth chakra (heart)

The third chakra (solar plexus)

The second chakra
(spleen and sex organs)

The first chakra (root)

Figure 1. The seven chakras. The energy works from the first chakra (at the base of the spine) up to the seventh (the crown chakra at the top of the head). Note that the sixth chakra (or the third eye) is located above the eyes in the center of the forehead. Readers should memorize these placements. (Figure adapted from *The Chart of the Mysterious Kundalini: The Location of the Glands*, published by Samuel Weiser as a poster.)

Nature has given us this wonderful form of energy—light and color—to sustain our minds and our bodies in perfect health. Health is the condition of perfect equilibrium, but can only be maintained as long as there is perfect rhythm and harmony throughout the body.

The whole basis of color healing consists of certain molecular reactions that take place in the organs through the medium of the rays. Light is not a force outside of us; light enters into the center of every cell, nerve, and tissue of the body. The beams of white light pay a fundamental part in the function and well-being of the inner body. When white light flows harmoniously into the interior centers (the chakras), our condition becomes healthy and more harmonious. When there is some obstruction in the chakra, blocks are formed, and these blocks prevent energy from flowing freely, and the body is unable to heal itself. Readers who are unfamiliar with the chakras should memorize them. (See figure 1 on page 3.)

In order to fully comprehend and use the power of the stones we are about to study, it is important to understand that all matter radiates light, and this is the light that causes the healing.

THE COSMIC LAW OF NUMBERS

There are certain laws in the universe that repeat themselves on many levels. Because each person is a small model of the universe—a microcosm in a macrocosm, made out of the same materials and governed by the same laws—it is important and necessary to understand two great cosmic laws: the Law of Three and the Law of Seven.

The Law of Three: All phenomena in every scale are the result of the meeting and the interaction of three principles or forces. According to Gurdjieff's teaching, nothing can happen without the interaction of a third principle or force. This same idea—that three forces are necessary for anything new to happen—was also found in many ancient teachings such as the original Christian doctrine of trinity; the Hindu teaching about the creation of the universe— from Brahman (the Absolute) arose Ishwara (the Creator), and through the joint action of Brahma, Vishnu and Shiva (the three different aspects of Ishwara) everything that exists was produced; the Sankga doctrine of the three gunas: raja, tamas, sattva. According to the Sankga philosophy, different combinations of these three principles, each with its characteristic quality, accounted for everything existing in the phenomenal world. Gurdjieff called these three forces active, passive and neutralizing.

The Law of Seven: Seven is the principal number of the planet Earth. It denotes transmutation: four (matter) + three (spirit). Their blending attains the supreme goal of human evolution. The Law of Octaves is an example of this manifestation.

The Egyptian priests left manuscripts showing their system of color science. They applied the law of correspondence between the seven-fold nature of man and the seven-fold division of the solar system. They taught that red, yellow, and blue corresponded to body, soul and spirit. It is a good classification which has been enlarged upon. They had certain color halls in their temples where the effects of color vibrations were studied and applied. The masses were not taught the full esoteric doctrine of light and color, but were given as much as they could assimilate. The Indian and Chinese mystics also had a knowledge of color in their secret doctrines. A list of the seven major rays is shown below.

1. Red   ⎫
2. Orange   ⎬   physical
3. Yellow   ⎭
4. Green
5. Blue   ⎫
6. Indigo   ⎬   spiritual
7. Violet   ⎭

THE ETHERIC BODY

The physical body consists of 1) the visible—dense or corporeal body (physical); and 2) the invisible—etheric double or vital body (prana). They function on the physical plane and are cast off by the human spirit at time of death. Until we realize that our ordinary senses respond to a very limited range of vibrations, and that outside there is a vast universe of life and activity, we cannot hope to unfold and develop our inner perception.

Matter, which appears solid, is not. It consists of atoms that are composed of electrons and protons. These are held together by electro-magnetic forces. Thus matter is composed of minute electric positive and negative charges. These are freely and orderly connected together by the invisible universal element called ether.

The ether is an omnipresent cosmic substance filling all space and is the medium by which all physical etheric forces contact the earth and ourselves. The vibrations of the ether are many and varied. Some of them are light, heat, color, electricity, etc.. Ether is the great connecting link between the physical senses and the higher cosmic forces.

The etheric body is about one and a half inches from the dense body and is a pale golden color. In cases of ill health, the natural treatment is to build up the exhausted forces of the etheric body by applying color vibrations to the appropriate centers. Color is the great cosmic healing force that works directly on the etheric cells, replenishing and revitalizing them. When I lay stones on the body it is the *etheric body* that is affected first and it then influences the gross or physical body.

THE AURA

The auric emanation, which consists of seven distinct waves of light encircling each individual in the shape of an egg, has the appearance of a luminous mist or cloud. The aura is the essence of your life. It reveals your character, emotional nature, mental ability, state of health and spiritual development. There are seven states in the aura. They are not separative states but they are the currents of thoughts and feelings flowing in the ocean of consciousness. They infiltrate and overlap with each other.

Physical {
1. Physical-etheric plane
2. Astral plane
3. Lower mental plane

4. Higher mental plane

Spiritual {
5. Spiritual-causal plane
6. Intuitive plane
7. Divine or absolute plane

The first four planes are concerned with ordinary existence and the remaining three belong to the spiritual.

The key is to be found in the nature of the species. We are septenary beings, evolving along seven planes of life. The seven-fold aura is the guide to our soul and character.

The aim of esoteric science of color is to build into the aura the seven pure rays—the seven jewels of the yogis—so body, soul, and spirit become revitalized, healed, transformed, and inspired from within.

ASPECTS AND APPLICATIONS OF COLOR

Each color has seven aspects: it vitalizes, animates, heals, enlightens, supplies, inspires and fullfills. The science of color has various applications:

1. A healing aspect in which color and stone treatment are used.

2. A psychological aspect which shows the influence of color on the mind and the emotions.

3. An esoteric aspect which is manifested in the symbology and attributes of colors and in the color aspects of the aura.

THE CHAKRAS

White light enters through the aura. Each of the seven rays infuses the appropriate soul-center or chakra with its particular quality. Each chakra absorbs a special current of vital energy, through its particular color ray from both the physical environment and from higher levels of consciousness. They are specialized channels of color force. They are the etheric organs working through thought and feeling directly upon the physical body. Table 1 shows how the seven rays correspond to the seven chakras.

Table 1. The Seven Rays and the Chakras

Color	Chakra	Quality
Violet	7. Crown (Pineal Gland)	Spirituality
Indigo	6. Third Eye (Pituitary Gland)	Intuition
Blue	5. Throat (Thyroid Gland)	Religious Inspiration
Green	4. Heart	Harmony, Sympathy
Yellow	3. Solar Plexus (Adrenals)	Intellect
Orange	2. Spleen or Sexual Organ	Energy
Red	1. Base of Spine	Life

Music

The Kundalini is music as it is color.
It is a rainbow as it is a perfect song.

Color and sound are aspects of vibration. Musical science is based upon the fundamental principle of the rhythm of the universe. Since these rhythms preceded the manifestation of the cosmos, it follows that music emerged with the first breath of divine creation.

Every sound emanates a certain color and takes on a definite form. Every form gives forth a sound; that sound is its keynote. Every created thing—from molecule to human being, from stone and plant to solar system—possesses a keynote of its own. The winds are tuned to certain rhythms as is the beat of the waves in the ocean. The sum total of all these notes make up the music of the spheres. The body temple is also an example: the beating of the heart, the flow of blood, the play of muscles, the pulsations of breath are all a part of this great body-symphony.

All stones emit sounds that have great potential for healing. The crystal, which is a powerful receiver and transmitter of electrical energy, emits sonic frequencies of a high vibratory rate. These have been heard by sensitives who call it "the music of the crystals." To those attuned to it, this music has the direct effect of lifting the consciousness to a higher level.

The music of crystals and stones, which is still relatively unknown, could inspire gifted musicians and healers in the expanding field of cosmic healing music. At this period of our evolution, we are discovering and realizing how music and sound can calm and heal the physical body as well as transform and induce qualities in the soul and spirit.

> Music is an art imbued with the power to
> penetrate into the very depth of the soul,
> imbuing us with the love of virtue.
> Plato

2 The Rainbow and the Seven Rays

THE RAINBOW

The rainbow reveals a wonderful mystery through the beauty and spiritual essence of the seven rays. In the spirits of the rays are centered all the potentialities of the highest dynamic powers and faculties. These hold the potentiality of absolute being. The rainbow is a cosmic proclamation of the divinity inherent in each of us. The gleaming spectrum of the rainbow reminds us that the color scale has the purpose to lift, to ennoble and to spiritualize all life. Communion with the soul of color lifts us beyond realms of matter, up into spheres of spirit and into cosmic space because light is universal and infinite.

Its message also states that a stage of evolution has been attained in which the human life wave has evolved a sevenfold body. Seven cosmic tones descend to earth in the seven notes of our diatonic scales. The rainbow bathes in sevenrayed color waves, whereby the so-called seven dormant jewels of the seven-fold body are being aroused. This merging of color and tone is a symbol of the kingdom of heaven within, in all its many ways.

In the Eastern tradition, there is a state called the rainbow body, which is achieved after much practice of yogic doctrine, in which the body (physical) is transmuted into the radiant body of glory. It is the highest body attainable, compared to *christos*. In the *body of glory* the master of yoga is said to be able to exist for aeons, possessed with the gift of appearing and disappearing at will in any one of the mansions of existence throughout the universe.

THE RAYS

The rays are spiritual forces emanating from the white light. They are perpetually vibrating—not only on the surface of the earth—but also above and through it, encircling the globe in streams of endless, inexhaustible energy.

As in the macrocosm so also in the microcosm, the same rays and forces surround and permeate every human being, flowing down the negative left side of the body and up the positive right side.

These great color vibrations are the real source of our powers, each one having a particular, as well as a general, function and purpose.

Each human being incarnates under a particular ray and is influenced by other subordinate rays. The focal point of the rays and vibrations is in the aura, the radiation of light that surrounds all creatures. Let us remember that we are always surrounded by color, which is a cosmic power and, therefore, a vital stupendous force. It works through us, in us, in every nerve, cell, gland and muscle. It shines in our auras and radiates upon us from the atmosphere. In essence color is spiritual.

THE TRINITY OF PRIMARY COLORS

The source (or Sun) contains within it practically everything of which the earth is composed. The colors of the spectrum are indicative of various metals and gases, given off in the forms of ether. Some are termed thermal and others cold or electric.

There are three primary colors unfolded in the white light: red, yellow and blue. These have a correspondence with the three basic elements hydrogen, carbon and oxygen. This three-fold power operates directly in furthering the growth and development of human beings physically, mentally and spiritually.

In the highest heaven-world, the ego manifests as a blue light, as it descends toward physical birth it becomes a yellow spark, in the third degree of its descent it takes on the vibration of red. The *blue ray* (cooling) is assimilated by the spiritual center in the head and awakens within a knowledge of its own inherent divinity. The *yellow ray* stimulates mental growth by way of the brain. The *red ray* (thermal) furnishes sustenance for the physical body, gaining entrance by way of the breath. The following principles correlate also:

We *will* in blue—WILL

We *think* in yellow—WISDOM

We *feel* in red—ACTIVITY

When blue is in harmony with yellow and red, there is peace and balance in body and mind. From this trinity emanate the secondary colors:

Orange combines red and yellow

Green combines yellow and blue

Indigo combines orange, green, blue and purple

Violet combines red and blue

The spectrum (or the seven rays) reveals to us the mysteries of the cosmos through the properties of each ray.

We need to apply that same relation to the stones to truly understand their healing magic. The stones carries the vibration of the particular color ray they are tuned to. In the next section each ray is correlated with its chakra and the stones which carry the chakra's vibration. The study and understanding of color is the basis for using the stones in a conscious way in order to heal. For example, as we think of the primary colors, associate with the following:

Blue . . . . . Spirituality . . . . . All blue stones
(sapphire, lapis lazuli, etc.)

Yellow . . . Wisdom . . . . All yellow stones
(amber, topaz, etc.)

Red . . . . . . Vitality . . . . All red stones
(coral, ruby, etc.)

THE SEVEN CHAKRAS, RAYS, AND STONES

First Chakra (Base of Spine)

All red stones: ruby, coral,
garnet, red jasper, bloodstone

Red is the symbol of life, strength, vitality and the physical nature. Experiments have shown that plants grown under red glass shoot up four times more quickly than in ordinary sunlight. Slower growth occurs under green and blue glass. Red obviously stimulates the vitality, whereas blue and green will slow it down. In nature, the color red is associated with heat, fire, anger, just as we "turn red" when we are in a state of passion or anger. Red is the color of fire. The red of terrestrial fire is transmuted into golden yellow (of pure spirit) as it rises. Red is the color of primitive types. Rose-red, however, is the color of universal harmony.

For healing, red is excellent in all blood deficiency diseases (such as anemia). It should be used when there is emaciation, when hands and face assume a blue tinge in cold weather, in deficient nutrition, depression, or lethargy. It is a healing and stimulating vibration.

Second Chakra (Spleen)

All orange stones: carnelian, fire opal,
*   orange jasper*

Orange is the symbol of energy. It is composed of red and yellow. Red symbolizes personality and yellow symbolizes wisdom. Therefore, through an integration of these two, we can overcome anger and establish self-control.

For healing, orange is essential for health and vitality. It is warm, positive, and stimulating, influencing primarily the vital problem of assimilation and circulation. It regulates the intake of food.

Third Chakra (Solar Plexus)

All yellow and golden stones: topaz,
*   citrine, amber*

Yellow is the symbol of mind, intellect, high intelligence, wisdom, the mental plane. It is a positive, magnetic vibration that has a tonic effect on the nerves. Because the solar plexus is the organizing brain of the nervous system, it is our "sun" or power center, and needs to stay in perfect equilibrium. Yellow, therefore, is the great equalizer for irritable conditions of the nervous system which unbalance the energy of the solar plexus.

For healing, yellow carries the power to cure diabetes and constipation. If someone is unusually lean or haggard, they probably draw in too much of the red ray, and yellow will help neutralize this condition in the system. For those who are too fat or phlegmatic, the blue ray has probably been overemphasized, and the yellow ray will help neutralize this as well.

Fourth Chakra (Heart Center)

All green stones: emerald, green tourmaline,
malachite, jade, chrysoprase, dioptase, peridot,
aventurine, moss agate, green jasper

Green is the symbol of harmony, sympathy, creativity, health, abundance, of nature in general. Green is the merging of yellow (soul) and blue (spirit). It appears in the spectrum at the point of color balance, between the first three rays (which are more concerned with the physical aspect) and the last three rays (which relate to the spiritual aspect). Green reaches outward in a horizontal manner, blue reaches upward in a vertical manner. Together they form the cross which is the symbol of life. This color, which is radiated everywhere in nature—in the fields, forests, grasses —restores tired nerves and gives new energy.

For healing, green has a balancing vibration that is important to the nervous system. It doesn't excite, inflame, or irritate. Because of its strong influence on the heart chakra, which is the center of the blood supply, green is a great aid to any heart problem or blood pressure disorder. It can always be used to restore tired nerves, and will help anyone who needs energy.

Although green is used primarily to create a more healthy vibration, some readers may also wish to work on the heart chakra with pink stones, as pink symbolizes softness, affection, and love. Some people may need to allow more softness and affection into the heart chakra, and if this is the case, you may wish to work with the following stones: tourmaline, rubellite, rhodochrosite, rhodonite, kunzite, or rose quartz.

Fifth Chakra (Throat Center)

All blue stones: sapphire, lapis lazuli, blue topaz, aquamarine, turquoise, chrysocolla

Blue is the symbol of inspiration, devotion, infinity, and religious aspirations. It lifts, exalts, and inspires one toward greater heights of endeavor and attainment. It produces a calm, peaceful radiation, which has sleep inducing qualities. The throat chakra is the focusing point of the spoken word. It is by means of this center that the indwelling spirit in each of us establishes communication with the outer world. The throat chakra is involved in expressing feelings.

For healing, the blue ray carries great curative power in regard to any disease or blockage in the throat. Because blue is associated with a lack of warmth, it is to be used when inflammation is present, or when any internal bleeding or nervous condition exists. It is cooling, sedative, astringent and healing. The deep dark blues indicate a power of tremendous intensity while the light blue (or azures) indicate high ethical inspiration.

Sixth Chakra (Third Eye or Pituitary Gland)

All indigo stones: indigo, sapphire, azurite

The indigo ray is the symbol of the mystical borderland—spiritual attainment, self-mastery, wisdom. This ray aids in the opening of the third eye (inner and outer vision), and it opens the doors to the subconscious. It can restore long buried soul memories. Indigo symbolizes the bridge between finite and infinite. It expels the negative elements of the consciousness, and helps build up the higher elements. It assists and guides our inner journey to cosmic knowledge.

For healing, it is of great value in the treatment of any mental disorder. It has also been used to help develop the third eye so that scientific and philosophic research can be done.

Seventh Chakra (Crown or Pineal Gland)

All violet stones: amethyst, fluorite

Violet is the ray of spiritual mastery. It is the highest and most subtle specialization of light, and corresponds with the highest elements in our nature. It stands at the crown of the spectrum in contrast to red. This highest vibration is a blend of red (matter) and blue (spirit), and the process of transformation can be painful. When working with the stones, keep in mind that the darker tones are associated with sorrow; deep purple signifies high spiritual attainment; pale lilac indicates cosmic consciousness and a love for humanity; bluish purple stands for transcendent idealism.

For healing, this stone is an aid for insomnia, or for any ailment that relates to mental disorders.

KEYS FOR USING COLORS AND STONES

In ancient times in Egypt and Greece, color temples were built into seven different compartments, each one containing one of the seven color rays. People were brought to these temples for both physical healing and spiritual uplifting. These ancient civilizations understood and used the power of the rays. Today we also need to be conscious that each of the seven great color manifestations affect particular centers of the body. Each color has a specific function to perform in the development of our lives. Color, like other forces in nature, is either positive or negative. Both the biological and the physical properties have to be understood and adapted to suit the particular individual that needs it at a particular time. For example, today I may need a red stone for vitality, but next week I may need to use a green one for harmony.

We are constantly surrounded by cosmic color, which helps us realize that as we ascend the ladder of spiritual attainment by developing mentally, morally and physically, we are also ascending in the degree of our sensitivity to light, color and stones.

Table 2 provides a key to using the rays and their related stones to restore nerves, and rebuild health for the physical, mental and spiritual plane.

Colors in the stones can be used in meditation to accelerate and awaken the power centers of the pituitary and pineal glands into activity. The following colors correspond to the spiritual centers for the head: indigo relates to

Table 2. Stones for Physical, Mental, Spiritual Conditions

Condition	Physical	Mental	Spiritual
Calming	Green stones	Indigo and green stones	Light blue stones, such as blue topaz and sapphire
Revitalizing	Orange stones	Emerald green stones or royal blue lapis lazuli	Golden and rose-pink stones
Inspiring and Stimulating	Red and pink stones	Yellow or golden stones such as topaz; also violet stones such as amethyst	Violet and purple stones

the pituitary, therefore an indigo sapphire would be of great benefit; violet relates to the pineal gland and an amethyst would be of great use and inspiration. A guide to using individual stones by color ray and chakra will be discussed further in Chapter 6.

WHITE AND BLACK

White and black symbolize creative activity. White symbolizes the presence of color, while black symbolizes its absence. There is a wonderful mystery in white and black which touches upon the deepest secrets of the universe. Ancient alchemists communicated many teachings about the contrasting forces of white and black, and the results that could be obtained by their fusion. Perfect balance of these two colors (or symbols) is known as polarity. Truth, too, is a polarity. When we reach this state of balance, a new earth will be created. When white and black merge, human evolution will reach its goal—divinity.

White is yang: it contains all the colors within it. White represents the masculine divine life essence; it is active, positive, all revealing, dynamic and stimulating. It symbolizes the cosmic day, supreme being. The powerful white ray is not so concerned with physical healing as it is with spiritual illumination. Its focus is the apex of the head, and the light enters through the pineal gland. White is used for protection of both the physical and mental body. There are instances when miraculous protection has been given by surrounding an individual with an aura of white light in times of emergency. White stones are: moonstone, opal, pearl.

Black is yin: it typifies the feminine and all form in general. Life essence must have form through which to manifest in order to become visible on the physical plane. It is negative (or feminine), passive, all concealing. It is the seed ground of infinity, the unmanifest, the unchartered. It symbolizes the cosmic night, the mysteries of incarnation, the abstract. The highest truths are revealed to those who have the courage to pass beyond all sight and sound, into the great darkness that precedes the light of the eternal, the void. "Darkness within Darkness is the Gate to all Mystery," says an old tao teaching. Black is ruled by Saturn, which, in its higher form, denotes the mysterious. That which is formless, working within, unperceived and unseen. The black stones are: black tourmaline, jet, smoky quartz, obsidian.

THE SIGNS OF THE ZODIAC AND COLOR—RELATED STONES

The human body is actually a constellation of the same powers that formed the stars in the sky. Although everyone contains the complete zodiac within on a symbolic level, some people may prefer to keep stones around them that relate to their astrological sun sign.

Aries (Red Stones)

The keynote of this sign is activity, which is manifested as initiative, ambition, or creativity on the physical plane—and spiritual adventuring or pioneering toward a better world for humanity on the higher plane. Aries people may run the entire gamut from red to its higher form—white—the lowest to the highest.

Taurus (Yellow and Pink Stones)

The symbols of this sign are love and wisdom. The true function of wisdom is illumination of the mind through the power of love. Taurus people are closely attuned to products of the earth. They need to transform the love of personal to

that of selfless service. Persistence and perseverance, qualities inherent in the spiritually awakened Taurean, will
transmute self-seeking into selflessness, or the tendency to
possessiveness into an impulse to share. Peace, plenty and
beauty become the soul signature of the illumined Taurean.

Gemini (Violet Stones)

Gemini is the sign of duality. It symbolizes life and death, joy
and sorrow, health and sickness, plenty and poverty. By
conservation and transmutation of the "serpent fire" within
the body, the law of alternation and death will be conquered.
That is the spiritual quest of this sign.

Cancer (Green Stones)

Cancer is termed the gateway to life. In the mystic waters
are born the seeds of life. Green is the color of the planet, of
nature. Life and love are synonymous in spiritual realms,
therefore new births on all planes of manifestation through
the magic power of love is the message and quest of this
sign.

Leo (Gold or Orange Stones)

Love is poured into the earth through the Sun. The Sun's
ray is gold. Gold is another way of expressing the orange
ray, for orange is a blend of the yellow ray of wisdom and
the red ray of activity. Leo symbolizes activity inspired by
wisdom. The heart (ruled by Leo) is the sun-center of light
for an illumined life. Divinity and humility are keynotes for
meditation for the native of this sign. The principal task of
slaying the lion of the self is a long and arduous process
that involves conflict that leads to an understanding that
love is fulfilling the law of life. It is loving understanding

between nations and individuals that will become the manifestation of this new age.

Virgo (Purple Stones)

The symbol of this sign is reason transforming itself to wisdom. Knowledge and understanding produce wisdom. Reason alone deals with externals—wisdom involves the inner heart. It is not possible to reach a state of illumination through reason alone—one must become wise.

Libra (Yellow Stones)

This is an airy sign related to the mind. Libra symbolizes an important turning point in nature, the autumn equinox. It signifies the trial we must all pass, the balance that must be weighed with the deeds of the year. It symbolizes the conquest of the lower separative self and the unfolding of love which leads to unity.

Scorpio (Red, Clear Crimson Stones)

One of the most powerful signs, Scorpio's force is dual in aspect, moving from the lowest depths to the greatest heights. Both the scorpion crawling on the ground and the eagle flying close to the Sun are symbolic of this sign. Transmutation is the key here, for the purification of the animal nature and the lifting of the forces to a higher plane of expression is Scorpio's task. By ruling our lower nature, we accomplish great power.

Sagittarius (Deep Blue Stones)

This sign is a symbol of animal man aiming toward potential godhood, for Sagittarius signifies high idealism and noble aspirations. It represents the number nine of initiation. A spiritualized mind is the highest expression for a Sagittarian.

Capricorn (Black and White Stones)

In this sign the mystery of the darkest night and the glory of the light merge. Capricorn symbolizes the crossing of the bridge of darkness before one can reach the radiation of the great white light. The conquest of the monster of the self is the goal.

Aquarius (Clear Blue Stones)

Natives of this sign are guided and lifted into new and undiscovered truths. They promote communication and group work. Their ideal is oneness of the whole, or wholeness of the one.

Pisces (Soft Blue and Indigo Stones)

This sign symbolizes the struggle of the spirit rescuing humanity from the monster of greed. Natives of this sign are drawn toward loving, selfless service, which is the only way to attain victory.

THE FOUR ELEMENTS IN THE ZODIAC

Fire, Earth, Air and Water are the four "vehicles" that are used in our progressive evolution. Each sign of the zodiac is assigned an element of its own. The elements that pertain to the signs are as follows:

> Fire Signs: Aries (red), Leo (orange-gold), Sagittarius (deep blue or purple blue) represent the pure flame of spirit.

Earth Signs: Taurus (yellow and pink), Virgo (clear violet), Capricorn (indigo, black and white) represent various phases of the physical body or "temple."

Air Signs: Gemini (deep violet), Libra (yellow), Aquarius (turquoise, indigo) represent the powers of the mind.

Water Signs: Cancer (green/silver), Scorpio (red), Pisces (blue) represent various aspects of the emotional nature.

A RAINBOW VISUALIZATION

Begin by seeing yourself totally surrounded by white light. Breathe in that light, bathe in it, hold it, become one with it.

Next you see waves of colors coming from deep within the earth. First you see and feel (in your first chakra) the primal fire, the red of blood, of life, of creation. As it rises toward the second chakra, it becomes the orange of the sun at sunset. It gives you energy. This fire of Shiva transforms itself into a brilliant yellow or gold as it enters the solar plexus (the third chakra). It is the shade of the sun at high noon. It gives you power—it is your own sun radiating. You feel your center. Your first three chakras, the lower body, are connected and receiving energy from the earth.

In the heart (the fourth chakra) you now see the emerald green of growth and creativity. You are reminded of your family—the plants, the trees. You feel harmony, tranquility, peace. Experience laying in grass—see yourself in a meadow.

Pouring down to you from the heavens, the blue ray centers your throat or fifth chakra. It reminds you of the vastness and infinity of the spirit and sky. It purifies your throat, your words. Next, the indigo ray enters the third eye (the sixth chakra) so you can go beyond the realms of reality and see truth. Finally, through the crown chakra (the seventh) the violet ray—a blend of earth and sky—helps you to understand your union with the cosmos. You are of spirit and body. Through this realization, you undergo transformation, merging the self with the one. This is the gate to enlightenment.

You experience your body as a rainbow body, lit up in these brilliant colors. You feel joy at seeing the luminosity, brightness and beauty of the rays. You bask in the wonder and magic of these forces.

The unique properties of the rays are your keys to knowledge and wisdom. By understanding the powers surrounding you, you are also able to understand the powers within you.

Let yourself fly and delve into the unknown, the unlimited, the undiscovered. May you become a sun-being, tuned to the love ray with the goal of creating a new world, a new age of light, peace, beauty, and harmony within and without.

3 The Mineral Kingdom

QUALITIES OF THE MINERAL KINGDOM

I come again from the mineral kingdom
To bring you riches of wisdom and Transmission of Light.

Ancient Shaman

There are three Kingdoms: the mineral kingdom, the plant kingdom, the animal kingdom. To become whole beings it is important and wise for each one of us to rediscover the living power existing in the forgotten and misunderstood mineral kingdom.

All energy comes from the one light and everything that exists has a vibratory rate. The minerals have the lowest vibrations of all living things. The mineral kingdom is the body of the earth; all that grows comes from it. We, too, come from the earth, and are made up of the same elements as the earth—we are not separate. In our search into the human soul, we discovered that matter has also been gifted with soul power.

The stones we are discussing in this book are significant entities—living, breathing, transmitting, interacting, shining, pulsating. They emit vibrations and frequencies that have very powerful potential effects on our whole being and can be used for healing, transforming, balancing, and attuning body, mind and spirit.

ANCIENT CONNECTIONS AND MESSAGES

As children we were always pulled by the magnetism of the stones, we brought them home to keep, to look at, to hold, to speak to. We let go of that connection with our mother earth, believing that it was child-like to have stones. As we grow in understanding and begin consciously applying ourselves to cleansing, transmuting and purifying body and spirit, we can rediscover a sensitive place in ourselves that responds to nature. It is our responsibility to rebalance and realign ourselves to the power of the elements, to our Mother Earth, our Father Sky, our Grandfather Fire and Grandmother Water. We are one great family.

Stones are manifestations of light and life, colors, textures, vibrancy, transparency, clarity. For me their beauty is magical, mystical, mysterious. They are the stars in the earth in which the qualities of clarity and light have been bestowed. This luminosity in the stone is a symbol of a high evolution. In the mineral kingdom there exists this aspect of spiraling growth, reaching for perfection, towards the light, just as in the plants the stalks grow upward—striving toward that same light.

PHILOSOPHER'S STONE: PRIMA MATERIA

Humanity has a common property referred to as *prima materia*. Its symbol is the philosopher's stone. It is the original substance, the ultimate principle of the world. According to this thought, all existing elements or phenomena are only variations of the same force or substance. These can be restored to purity by reducing and dissolving the manifold qualities, which have imposed themselves upon it through differentiation and specialization. Therefore, if we succeed in penetrating to the purity of the substance's undifferentiated primordial form, we have gained the key to the secret of all creative power. This is based on the mutability of all elements and phenomena. Transmutation is the key.

The patterns in the stones tell us of the changes, of the growth, layer upon layer of thousands of years. They give us the message that life is change—that the process of evolution is a cosmic law. The stones have crystallized through this heat and pressure, and they receive powers from the different planets based on the different color rays. Each stone is tuned into a particular ray and has a particular function and purpose to serve. Their formation is a sacred process that still remains a secret—even to the scientists who try to explain it. It is not my aim to delve into the different substances that make up the stones because that would still not explain their power. I let the stones keep their mystery and their sacredness. Acceptance of their power through your own personal experience with them is all that is necessary.

CHOOSING A STONE

It is important to open your heart to the stones. Trust your intuition and your feelings. Don't use your mind to explain or rationalize them. You may wish to have a stone that is tuned to your zodiac sign, but don't limit yourself to only that stone. Let your higher self guide you to the stone that you need *now* because of its particular color or properties. As you ponder your choice, one or two stones may call your attention strongly. These are the ones that need to go with you.

CLEANSING THE STONE

Once you have chosen a stone (actually it chooses you), it is important that you clean it, wash and purify it. Because of its high sensitivity, it carries vibrations and other imprints which need to be cleansed and purified, especially if you have received a stone from someone in your family who has been ill, or who has passed on. The stones cannot harm you, but the thoughts of others, which are attached to the stone, can cause harm.

If you are cleaning crystal quartz, you may wash it in water to which you have added sea salt. However, for all other stones, I recommend that you cleanse them in water, earth or fire. You can leave the stone under running water for six to eight hours, for a really thorough cleansing. Or you may bury it in some earth overnight, and then rinse it off. You may wish to cleanse a stone by fire—and putting the stone in the flame of a candle is the easiest way to do this. (Please don't burn yourself in the process!) You may even wish to have your stone repolished, especially if it has become dull or lost its lustre. Another way to clean and purify any stone is to put it in a large cluster of quartz for several days. It will revive its energy from the contact.

After you have washed your stone, put it in direct sunlight. Your stone will be very appreciative of this care. The sun is a great source of energy and purification. It is necessary to do this process regularly. Keep clean thoughts to protect yourself from the negative thoughts that come back to us like boomerangs. That is the reason why so many stories or myths about unlucky stones developed. It is not the stone but the thoughts and the intent that have carried these negative energies. It is the consciousness of the wearer that has contributed to these tales. Give yourself an affirmation that your stone is now clean of impure thoughts, that it is ready to help you with its light, that you embrace it as your ally or power nature friend. Thank it, use it, wear it, love it! Know that you and your stone are fullfilling an evolutionary cycle.

OLD AND NEW STONES

There are old stones and young stones. The earth is constantly replenishing and balancing herself. Sometimes I cried when I went to the mines and saw how our Mother Earth was being raped because of the greed for precious stones. But I received a message: the stones are gifts to us, to be used consciously, to be loved and respected, and the earth is producing new stones to realign herself. This is to benefit our process of development towards illumination. The earth is rich and abundant; she keeps giving. Let us balance this by adopting an attitude of gratitude and responsibility toward our first kingdom—the mineral kingdom.

UNITY IN DIVERSITY

In the summer of 1983 I was invited to attend the "Second International Gathering of Shamanism and Healing" in Alpbach, Austria. It was a blessed event. On the first morning, as I sat in a sacred circle with shamans and healers of different colors, nationalities, origins and beliefs, I was reminded of my friends, the luminous stones. They teach us that light of different colors come to shine together to demonstrate the oneness in all. The various paths are different modes of arriving at the same central point. There is unity in diversity.

All these shamans and healers were carriers of ancient knowledge. They were ready to share it openly in a consciously positive manner. They shared in common a belief and a respectful attitude towards the elements, the great family of earth, fire, air, water and ether. They used (and understood) the powers of the stones and encouraged me on this path.

To return to the roots, to bring this ancient wisdom into a "present" which is integrated and whole is the responsibility of this Age:

I am older than the body
And I come again
In Music of the Crystals
Heart of Rubies
Seed of Pearl
Tongue of Lapis
Eyes of Fire Opal

4 The Quartz Crystal

POWER AND QUALITIES OF THE CRYSTAL

The clear quartz crystal, also known as mountain crystal or rock crystal, is one of the most sacred stones if not the most sacred of ancient and present cultures.

It is the essence of rocks, the highest expression of the mineral kingdom. It is found in mountains and rocks. It is sometimes more clear and transparent than water. Objects can be seen as clearly through it as in a mirror. It catches the light and reflects beautiful rainbows. It is a symbol of radiant white light energy.

If you have a crystal, please get it at this time. Let it be by your side, observe it, feel it, establish a relationship with it as you read this chapter.

The quartz crystal is a symbol, a mirror of our soul. It represents our struggle for clarity. The bottom of the crystal is usually dense, opaque. As it grows through countless struggles, it gets clearer and clearer. We, too, strive to achieve clarity of purpose and of being after our various struggles.

Its power lies also in its structure, growing, reaching up toward the light, from the depths of the earth. Its apex (which is the point at the crown where the six sides meet) is like a pyramid, representing the forces of trinity, doubled.

The more pointed the apex, the more perfect its healing power, which can be used as a laser beam. For this purpose three sides should touch.

The quartz crystal acts as a catalyst, a conductor of energy. It is both a receiver (or receptor) and a transmitter. It is a protective ally that balances and harmonizes the aura, giving it equilibrium. Crystals attune themselves automatically to human vibrations because of their affinity with the human spirit, creating spiritual links when they are worn or held. Remember to wash your crystal and keep it clean so it can protect you from outside negative vibrations.

How the Crystal is Used

The uses of the clear quartz crystal are unlimited in both the healing field and the scientific or industrial field. In Atlantis and Lemuria, they were used as highly evolved tools because of the purity of their light beam and their ultrasonic transmitting power, much as today's electronic world and industry use them. In Egypt they were used in the pyramids to attract the power of light. They were well understood because of their shape and structure, which is expressed in triangles.

In Europe, during the war, they were used as amplification devices. Crystals were put next to wires when lines of communication were broken. To the American Indian culture it has been, and remains, their most sacred stone, a symbol of light in the earth. In some tribes, the baby's cord is cut with a crystal, which, of course, establishes the connection with the earth and light right from birth. The crystal is used in their homes during ceremonies and rituals, and is buried with the dead.

It is used in much the same way, and treated with the same respect in the culture of Tibet. These two cultures understood and kept these beliefs of the sacredness of the earth and the stones, and the powers in the elements. And so both the American Indian and the Buddhist of Tibet often carry on their body a quartz crystal for protection and illumination. The American Indian wears a little pouch around his neck which contains a crystal, perhaps a turquoise and/or coral, herbs and whatever else he believes to carry power. The Tibetan wears a little pouch around his waist or leg. It contains a crystal, other sacred stones and a little rolled paper in which a prayer is written, perhaps a mantra.

The quartz crystal is itself a force field of light and energy which can be used as a sonic protection against negativity. This property exists in all sizes of crystals including the small ones we wear or carry. The passage of ions through the molecular structure makes them a valuable aid in clearing and neutralizing negative conditions in the aura of people of all ages. It can be used to cleanse the atmosphere of larger areas, such as our homes or places of work, as well.

It can become our own personal healer for the body as well as a tranquilizer and transformer for the spirit. It helps our intuitive insight, to see the light in the darkness, to be our own light. When laid on the body the Crystal Quartz decrystallizes the knots which block the flow of energy.

SELF HEALING WITH CRYSTALS

You and a friend may give each other a crystal massage. Make sure you wash it in sea salt water first, then wipe it dry with a clean cotton cloth. Begin by lying down on your stomach. The crystal should be fairly small. Start with the bottom of the feet, poke gently with the point and rub with its side. Do one leg first, then the other, then up the back being careful of the spine, neck, back of the head, arms, hands. Then ask the person to turn over and begin the process again at the feet, all the way up. As you approach the solar plexus make a circular motion with the crystal, clockwise to help decongest that area. Be gentle near the heart chakra because we all carry pain there. You may finish by giving the face and head massage, rubbing the crystal on the forehead, cheekbones, out into the hairline. You will feel refreshed, renewed and revitalized.

Another method is to give yourself an aura balancing treatment by laying crystals on each of the chakras. If you do not have enough, place one on your solar plexus, heart and third eye centers. Your arms should be beside your body with the palms of your hands facing up in a receiving position. Close your eyes, take deep breaths and relax. Let whatever images come. Do not suppress your feelings. However, don't leave the crystals on your body for more than twenty to thirty minutes.

CRYSTAL MEDITATION

A crystal is a wonderful tool for meditation. It helps tune our consciousness to the source. It aids us in taking the quantum leap that attracts our soul toward the light. Here are some suggestions for meditation:

1. Lie down on your back and put one quartz crystal on your third eye. Be as receptive and open as possible to what you may experience. Don't hold yourself back from a fantasy journey or an imaginary world. Pass through the gates—a crystal palace or a crystal cave awaits you! Don't leave the crystals on the third eye for longer than fifteen to twenty minutes.

2. If you are doing a group meditation, put the quartz crystal in the center of a circle of people and

use it as a point of focus—a reference point of earth and light.

3. You can also prepare an altar using the four elements: light a candle (fire); have a bowl of water or a vase of flowers (water); light incense (air); and put your crystal in front of you (earth). Sit quietly, looking at the crystal, then gently close your eyes, keeping the image of the crystal in your third eye. Give thanks and focus on clarity. Because it is a symbolic aspect of the Self, getting in touch with the quartz crystal helps you get in touch with the inner Self! It strengthens the third eye, or your ability for "seership."

• • •

When the process of meditation, the meditating self and the object of the meditation combine and merge into one, this is called meditation. Perfect concentration is meditation. Truth is revealed at that stage. All knowledge resides within the individual, but it does not come up to consciousness because external training exercises such a great influence over the brain that it blocks the knowledge within us, and we are not able to remember what we "know." So long as our minds remain extroverted, they cannot be introverted. With an extroverted mind, it is not possible to acquire knowledge—that is why certain meditation practices are required. External objects can be used as an aid to awaken this power, however.

In the practice of tratak, which is a yogic crystal gazing meditation, we can even predict past and future events. It is a long and difficult process which requires much discipline. We train ourselves to be in complete concentration, gazing at the crystal steadily in such a way that we do not see anything else. Later, as we progress we will detect forms. It is then that we need to be critical and searching in regard to what is seen.

CEREMONIAL USES

In the Far East a long time ago, priests would go to look and find a lump of crystal in the Himalayas. They would carefully chip off the rough edges and through years and years would carve the piece of rock into spherical shape. Then generation after generation of priests would polish the crystal by using finer and finer sand and water. Finally the crystal would be ready for religious use, seeing the future, seeing the will of the gods.

In Africa the shaman's bag for bones, which he throws to find out how to deal with the problems of an individual, much as we throw cards for divinatory purposes, contains a crystal to symbolize light and water.

In various parts of Ireland, little crystal balls are set in silver rings. They are believed to attract favorable responses from the Irish leprechauns, who are nature spirits.

During a full moon it is a propitious time to perform a ceremony with your crystal. It is an American Indian tradition that was taught to me and which I like to practice. Just as the full moon rises, you may go up a hill and take your crystal (or crystals) on a plate or in a bowl resting on herbs, such as cedar or sage. Light the herbs as incense and offer the crystal to the Moon, chanting and praying, giving your thanks. Then take the crystal and beam it, by directing its rays to yourself, your body and your companions. It has been charged with the light and power of the moon.

To carry your crystal, it is best to wrap it in either cotton, silk or velvet. Please do not use synthetic fabrics. Keep the color of the cloth as neutral as possible so as not to influence the clear vibrations of the crystal. Raw silk is a superb choice. Crystals radiate their light best on black velvet.

THE CRYSTAL PENDULUM

I use a crystal pendulum for decision making as well as for checking energies in a person's body when I am giving a treatment. The pendulum has become my ally, my friend. I trust it totally. I realize that it is my higher self, my higher guidance that comes through it. We all need to remember that it is to the degree that we are open and receptive that we will reap the benefits.

> Let the Great Light in the Crystals
> Come into your heart
> And illuminate your soul!

VARIETIES OF CRYSTALS

There are several varieties of crystal quartz: smoky quartz, rutilated quartz, and tourmaline quartz. (Other members of the quartz family, such as rose quartz, amethyst, and citrine quartz will be discussed later.) If a quartz crystal contains inclusions of water or air, it is called a rainbow quartz because of the colors contained within. If another crystal is growing inside it, it is called a phantom quartz.

Smoky Quartz

This is a clear crystal with a dark smoky color. It is very powerful and the darkness in it is not negative, but represents the mysterious. This crystal, sometimes called smoky topaz, can help shift levels of consciousness from lower to higher. It is a serious stone, very earthy in its character, and it helps sharpen abstract thinking. Its scope of healing is limitless because it emits an ultrasonic frequency that creates tremendous healing—like an invisible laser beam—cutting through much of our density. I have one smoky crystal that I use in healing. I need only to beam it—it doesn't even touch the skin of the people that I work with— and yet they feel its electrical charges immediately. It carries a Saturnian influence of stability and responsibility, yet it relaxes and sedates. It represents the unconscious, the yin, the feminine, the left side, the intuition (when clarity is seen through the darkness). We think that in Atlantis it was used as a focal point of energy in trace training, and in this life it helps us go into the deepest and darkest parts of ourselves to bring out into the light the power symbolized by the stone.

Rutilated Quartz

This is a clear crystal that contains rutile fibers that have a golden or reddish color. These fibers add even more intensity and transmission power to the crystal because they bear cross currents of electrical charges that amplify healing. The difference between the lighter shades (of silver) and the more warm intense shades (of gold and red) *do* affect the vibration, as silver is quieter and the gold and red relate to more intense feelings. The inclusions in the stone are highly valuable. Sometimes they make beautiful patterns and symbols, which hold magnetic force fields. The key to its powerful healing energy lies in the projection of the electrical currents that can transmute disturbances in the body, by aiding in the building of healthy cells and tissue of infected organs. Because of its golden color, it may be used on the solar plexus to relieve anxiety and fear, or to aid in giving it eqilibrium and power. I also like to use it on the heart, if the heart feels especially sad or weak. It is a great balancing and healing agent.

Tourmaline Quartz

This clear quartz with needles of black tourmaline has doubled power. The combined forces of the clear crystal and the black tourmaline work on the universal law of opposites and polarity. It represents the yin and the yang within us. It aids in letting go of old conditioned patterns that are destructive to growth and development. It realigns and rebalances the aura. The tourmaline is highly electrical and sensitive. More information on the tourmaline is presented on page 64.

The Diamond

The diamond is the highest expression of the white light— the universal light. It is the emperor of stones, the most precious and powerful. It is the highest symbol of clarity, purity, illumination. It represents the pure focus of energy emanating from the will aspect of divinity. It helps to harmonize the heart and the will with divine mind, creating the trinity of perfection.

All seven rays blend into the cosmic unity of the one and the diamond contains all the attributes and qualities toward a perfected state in the mineral kingdom. It is the gem with the highest potency and its functions are unsurpassed. Unlike other stones, the diamond is a coal which, through countless polishings and facetings, acquires its incredible brilliance. We, too, can learn from that process.

The diamond carries great healing power. It cures most illnesses and is a great protector against negative vibrations and thoughts. The diamond is hard and sharp; it cuts off all arbitrary conceptions and leads us to the other shore of enlightenment.

The Buddha talked about reaching a state of illumination, or enlightenment. He referred to it as the diamond mind or enlightened mind. The diamond has pure transparency and reflection which cuts through all, yet nothing cuts through it. It is a jewel symbolizing the highest transformation, starting as coal and becoming a multi-faceted brilliant gem. The facets (which allow the light to come in and reflect from all sides) give a feeling of opening many windows, shining from everywhere.

There exists a state of consciousness in its undivided purity, no more split into the duality of subject and object. It is infinite, it has overcome the dualism of ego and non-ego. The purity of this state of consciousness is referred to as radiating toward all sides, penetrating everything with light. This is the consciousness in the state of enlightenment. Those who have realized this have truly found the Philosopher's Stone, the precious jewel.

. . .

There once lived a king in India who was very proud of his wealth. A yogi said to him, "Do not let yourself be blinded by your present riches." The King said, "Give me advice which I can follow according to my own nature and capacity—without changing my outer life and I will accept it." The yogi knew of the king's fondness for jewels, so he chose the king's natural inclination as a starting point and as a subject for meditation—thus in accordance with tantric usage, turning a weakness into a source of strength. "Behold the diamonds of your bracelet, fix your mind upon them and meditate thus: they are sparkling in all the colors of the rainbow; yet these colors which gladden your heart, have no nature of their own. In the same way imagination is inspired by multivarious forms of appearance, which have no nature of their own. The mind alone is the radiant jewel, from which all things borrow their temporal reality." And the king, while concentrating upon the bracelet on his left arm, meditated as he was told by the yogi, until his mind attained the purity and radiance of a flawless jewel. He had become the diamond.

• • •

The person who has found the Philosopher's Stone, the radiant jewel of the enlightened mind within his or her own heart, transforms mortal consciousness into that of immortality and perceives the infinite in the finite. This is the teaching of the diamond vehicle of the Tibetan Buddhist.

We are all diamonds, but as yet uncut and unpolished. We have many processes to go through before we reach a state of beauty and perfection. Let us not resent these processes, but be grateful for each and every one of them for they will help us to reach the goal—the perfected state of illumination.

5 Using Precious Stones

INTRODUCTION

We are traveling together,
The Path is long
It is strewn with
Bones and Precious Stones.

Since ancient times, stones have been believed to have psychic powers. These exert a great influence upon all aspects of our lives. The stones are alive—entities pulsating, radiating, vibrating at different rates. They create strong energy fields which enable us to be charged with their energies; they activate our abilities, soothe and comfort, heal and balance through the purity and directness of their beams. They express through their facets our infinite variety of aspects.

Illumination is the key word for the Stones
They illuminate the Earth as Stars do
They have light and shine, even when unpolished
They contain the seed of light, the point of light
The Center of the Cosmic Sea.

The colors are rays of love. Each has its own particular vibration. By understanding the unique properties of each of the seven rays we will be able to apply these same qualities to the stones. The study of colors is a preparation to using stones in a healing and spiritually transformative way. The stone emits the magnetic power of the ray of light contained within. The aura is benefited and the whole being feels more harmonious. Let us review:

- Reds and oranges are stimulating and invigorating to the physical body;

- Yellows vitalize and accelerate mental activities;

- Greens are calming and soothing to the nervous system;

- Blues and indigo are inspirational, giving spiritual tone;

- Purples accelerate and sublimate all processes of body, mind and spirit.

COSTUME JEWELRY

Beauty aids, creams and cosmetics were made from a paste of stones. They were used to paint the eyes, mouth and face. Malachite, Egypt's favorite stone, was used by the high priestesses as a cosmetic for their eyes and hair. Also the ruby was used to redden the mouth or face. The deep blue of the lapis was used on eyelids.

The beauty of precious stones is imcomparable—which is why they are so prized in jewelry. Since the beginning of time on this planet, stones have been used to enhance and adorn the body, the clothes and the environment. In many cultures, the stone cutters (the lapidaries) were knowledgeable about the hidden and mystical properties of stones. Many were apothecaries, alchemists or high priests who used their powers to make jewelry to protect, to symbolize, to represent, to attract, to dispel or to heal. Unfortunately as the wise ancient ones were replaced by more less knowledgeable people these secrets were forgotten or put aside. The stones kept their beauty, of course, but they stopped talking because we stopped listening. They lay dormant waiting to be reawakened to their true purpose and mission.

The high priests and priestesses of Egypt, who were usually also healers, wore many stones on their bodies, heads and hands, to charge themselves or to beam power at their patients. From Egypt comes this ancient poem:

> My God Thoth is of precious stones
> He lights up the Earth with his sparkle
> The Moon disc on his head is of red Jasper
> His phallus is of Quartz.
>
> Thoth I fear nothing
> Since you became my strength.

Precious stones and gems of great beauty are used in the crowns of kings, queens, and religious leaders for the same purpose of charging them as a battery. These leaders were believed to be symbols of divinity on earth. The Tibetan Buddhist believes in five sacred stones: the crystal for light; the turquoise for infinity of sea and sky; the coral for life and form; gold for the golden ray of the sun; and silver for the light of the moon. Amber and the carnelian are often used in their jewelry or charmboxes. The American Indian also has great reverence for these stones. The turquoise is worn for protection and is believed to hold the atmosphere of the world. The coral is worn for life and blood force. It is amazing to me that these two cultures (the Tibetan and the American Indian), which are located so far from each other, have so many of the same customs. They both respect and love the earth. They are connected to the magic and power of everything that is alive, knowing that everything has a soul and a vibration. They believe and trust that the elements in nature are our ancestors, and that they should be consulted for advice.

The records of the early Christian writers reveal a belief that the stones in the breastplate of the high priest were so highly magnetized by their respective planetary rulers that the stones were capable of responding to questions in flashing color language.

During the reign of Charlemagne, there was a great mystical movement in existence. Those connected with it saw the light of the stones as a symbol of spirit in matter. Charlemagne's crown was covered with precious stones so that his crown chakra would receive energy and be charged with the power of the stones. As a king he was believed to represent God on earth. Another example of the mysticism with stones is St. Stephan's recicario. This purse, or box, is completely covered with gems. It contains earth mixed with the blood of this martyr-saint who was stoned to death.

GEMS AND THE ZODIACAL RULERS OF THE DAYS OF THE WEEK

The Hermetic brotherhood observed strict rules relating to the use of precious stones. Table 3 shows the days and their corresponding planetary affinities. Like the Hermetic brotherhood, you may wish to work with certain stones on certain days. You may also be drawn to a stone that represents the day of the week on which you were born.

Table 3. Correlation of Gems to the Days of the Week

Day	Planetary Ruler	Gem
Sunday	Sun	Gold and yellow gems (amber, gold topaz)
Monday	Moon	All white stones (pearls, moonstones)
Tuesday	Mars	All red stones (rubies, garnets, etc.)
Wednesday	Mercury	All blue stones (turquoise, sapphire, lapis lazuli)
Thursday	Jupiter	All purple stones (amethysts)
Friday	Venus	All green stones (emeralds, malachite)
Saturday	Saturn	All black and white stones (diamonds, smoky quartz, etc.)

STONES COMBINED WITH ZODIACAL SIGNS AND COLORS

All minerals and gems are attuned to the constellations and proclaim their affinity by their color. Anyone possessing or wearing jewels will attract the planetary force to which the gem is related by nature. Hence the great importance of wearing jewels in harmony with your stellar rays.

Table 4. Zodiacal Signs, Gems and Color Rays

Sign	Gems	Color
Aries ♈	Ruby, Bloodstone, Red Jasper	Red
Taurus ♉	Golden Topaz, Coral, Emerald	Yellow
Gemini ♊	Crystal, Aquamarine	Violet
Cancer ♋	Emerald, Moonstone	Green
Leo ♌	Ruby, Amber	Orange
Virgo ♍	Pink Jasper, Turquoise, Zircon	Violet
Libra ♎	Opal, Diamond	Yellow
Scorpio ♏	Garnet, Topaz, Agate	Red
Sagittarius ♐	Amethyst	Purple
Capricorn ♑	Smoky Quartz, Beryl, Jet	Blue
Aquarius ♒	Blue Sapphire	Indigo
Pisces ♓	Diamond, Jade, Aquamarine	Indigo

Birthstones conduct the energy that each cycle and season brings. It is also wise to wear a stone that will support whatever is a critical or a weak point in your horoscope. Table 4 lists the stones that relate to the signs.

EFFECTS OF WEARING GEMS

The more precious stones you wear, the more strongly you will be charged with cosmic forces, which radiate out into your surroundings.

Sometimes the stones draw disease, pain and misfortune out of the etheric body of the person who wears them. Ruby and coral fade when people have anemia. Other stones, such as turquoise, lose or change color when the wearer is not well (either physically or psychically). Sometimes other stones give their power to their wearer—such as topaz, emerald, and diamond. Some stones have vibrational frequencies, which can inspire spiritual awakenings, or which help us become more responsive to the concept—such as the amethyst or the indigo sapphire.

Wear your stones. Don't shut them away in a safe or jewelry box. Don't deprive your soul and your body of this tremendous power that has been bestowed upon us.

If you wear rings, please make sure that the stones are set directly on the skin, as they give you more power that way.

People often ask me about the value of the difference between cut and polished stones, and stones in their raw state. Some serve well both ways—cut or uncut. However, some need to be cut and polished to bring out their functions. The garnet truly serves when it is cut, polished and sometimes faceted. Contrary to this, the amethyst serves best in its raw crystal form. There are no rules; one needs to be with the stone, and to experience the stone, in order to really understand it. Polishing is an art. The artisan must be an artist in order to bring out the most light and beauty from the faceting of the stone. The diamond is proof of the sensitivity required in faceting a stone.

When you purchase a stone, try not to worry too much about its cost. It is better to spend money to prevent sickness, or to align and balance yourself than to spend it on medications and doctor bills once you become ill! You can also achieve great benefits from semi-precious stones which are not as costly as rare gems. However, we need to realize that precious stones, such as rubies, emeralds, and sapphires, have pàrticular magical properties.

The following alternative stones, which are sold in mineral shops, are all capable of bestowing the qualities and properties of the ray needed. Examples are:

Crystal quartz can replace diamonds

Garnets can replace rubies

Lapis lazuli or sodalite can replace blue sapphires

Turquoise or chrysocolla can replace aquamarine

Citrine can replace topaz

Carnelian can replace the fire opal

Rhodochrosite can replace rubellite (the pink tourmaline)

Malachite or chrysoprase can replace emeralds

Azurite can replace the indigo sapphire

Please be open and receptive about the stones. Let the stones pick you, and let your highest guidance direct you to do what you need to do at that moment.

MYSTICAL ASPECTS

The ancients believed that every gem was crystallized by and around an entity. This entity was able to influence the wearer as to coming events, thereby enabling him to avoid danger or to embrace opportunity. Those who made use of these hidden powers in the gems made talismans, which were magnets of great potency. They were capable of transmitting powers that would help restore health and well-being. They were also able to convey forces carrying destruction through the negative intent. Forces can be equally used for the highest good or for the most evil and selfish purposes! It is the consciousness in the soul that needs to be transformed, in order to use the energy for good purpose.

The stones can be carved with a particular symbolic shape or form—such as a circle, cross, triangle, square, or spiral—to gain added potency. In Egypt, the scarab (which signifies eternity) was often carved in lapis lazuli or turquoise for the double power of infinity. The scarab is the animal that rides the eternal sun, and turquoise and lapis lazuli (both blue stones) symbolize the infinity of the sky and spirit. In the Mohammadan culture, one often saw letters for the name of Allah (or God) carved on carnelian or lapis lazuli. The vibrations of the stones have the inherent potential to heal, energize, attune and uplift the spirit of the inner being. Because they create such strong energy fields, stones were used to charge religious objects, altars, temples and places of worship, as well as being used at ceremonies.

These cosmic powers are everywhere, and they only need to be focussed, transformed, and used as magnets (or receivers) to help the individual along the spiritual path. The more we open ourselves up to the stones (and the cosmos), the more we will receive. Our lives will become abundant and we can feel joy about being part of this life.

In Chapter 4, I mentioned doing a full moon ceremony, but you don't have to limit yourself to just that. You may like to do a ceremony at solstice or equinox times, for these indicate changes in seasons, and during this time the atmosphere is charged with great power. Ceremonies and rituals can be used to reconnect with the power of the elements. They are our links to the ancient ones and to the cosmos. By participating in this kind of a ceremony, we are dedicating and devoting time to the higher in us—the mystical and the spiritual. We can step out of this present reality and consciously create a magical environment where we can transcend all images of the self and the world for a moment. It is through this rediscovery of the sacred that our

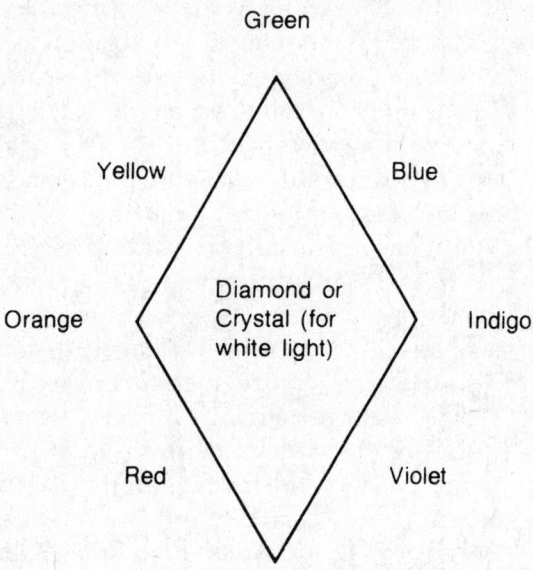

Figure 2. A mandala of stones. To prepare your mandala, put a quartz crystal or diamond in the center, and surround it with a stone for each of the seven rays. For the red ray, use garnets, dark rubies or red jasper. For the orange ray, use carnelian, fire opal, or orange jasper. For the yellow ray, use citrine, topaz, or amber. The green ray can be made from malachite, jade, or emeralds, while the blue ray is composed of either lapis lazuli, sodalite or sapphires. The indigo ray should be made from azurite or an indigo sapphire. The violet ray can be made by using an amethyst or flourite. This mandala is also shown in color as Plate 4 on page 90.

minds and hearts can joyfully come together in praise and gratitude.

If you carry your stones, musical instruments, and offerings out into the open spaces, you can celebrate the solstice or the equinox more joyfully. Bring companions and rejoice in the beauty and bounty of this earth! You will be given riches that you cannot touch with your hands—for your heart and soul will be fed. Your spirit will be lifted by joyous chants. Sing!

It is also very important that you create a quiet space in your home where you can go regularly to replenish yourself. This is important for self-centering. In this place you may want to build an altar that contains the four elements previously mentioned, and perhaps a mandala of stones, as shown in figure 2.

You can use this mandala as part of a visualization exercise in your private place. After you set up the stones, visualize yourself at the center of Divine White Light, surrounded by the Seven Cosmic Rays coming through the stones, and charging you with their healing light.

Beauty can be used to lift your emotions beyond yourself. See nature's light in these forms of life, for the precious stones, or gems, have a way of healing the emotions that have been inharmonious. The radiation of the rays of the stones will work deeply at reharmonizing any area filled with congested energies.

Each life we live is a "gem" or a step toward the necessary development of divine qualities. The stones can be utilized for spiritual rebirth. They can heal and uplift the soul, so dwell on their beauty and harmony, rather than dwelling on greed because you own them. It is important to realize that all we have is just borrowed, and it will all go back to the source.

The more we lose our ego, the greater becomes the clarity and radiance of our being. By working with the source, we can also help others. The faculty of light, or enlightenment, is inherent in every living being.

HEALING ASPECTS

The stones' frequencies are pulled by the etheric body through the chakras (also referred to as light centers or jewels) to replenish, revitalize, realign whatever is needed. It is through the power and intensity of the light that healing is achieved. The clearer—or more brilliant—the light, the more healing or transformative is its power.

There are many stones that are not called healing stones, but that have wonderful quality. They remind us of the earth. Fill your home with stones. Some will come to you from foreign lands you visit, some will be gifts, and some may be purchased because of your attraction to their color. Surround yourself with them. Your plants like them, too. Put stones on your plant pots. They appreciate and recognize each other.

> Let the Beauty of the Stones
> Speak to you
> The sparkling light
> In the gem of the Heart and Mind

There is a myth from the orient about the "wish granting gem." Like Aladdin's magic lamp, it grants any desire that its possessor formulates.

> Look deeply into the gem of your heart
> What is the wish hidden there?
> Listen to your inner world—
> It will reveal the secret there.

I heard:

> Be gentle yet strong,
> Be open and kind,
> Be beautiful and shine,
> Be the Jewel in the Lotus.

6 The Stones

Beauty is Truth, Truth is Beauty,
That is all ye know on Earth,
and all ye need to know.

Keats

This chapter defines the stones. They have been listed by color, starting with the red stones, and working on toward the violet hues. We also discuss the value of black and white stones. If you want to look up the definition of a particular stone, please see the index for easy reference.

RED STONES

Ruby

The ruby—clear red—fires up the heart with sparkles. The emotion known as love must be lifted to one of selflessness towards the light of universal love, to compassion for all life. The light in the heart illuminates the whole being as in the illuminati. It symbolizes the heart of spiritual love and devotion through the forces of purification and transfiguration. It is connected to Shiva, which is also an aspect of divine fire and purification. The red of terrestrial fire is transmuted into the golden yellow of pure spirit essence. Its fire inspires the love of truth and wisdom, transmuted to divine wisdom.

The ruby gives positive life force qualities. It activates and vitalizes the whole body through the circulation of the bloodstream. It has a heating and stimulating vibration. Sometimes it contains inclusions of rutile needles, which give it a silky lustre and added power.

Honor and value this gem for its life and love giving energy, for compassion is needed throughout our planet earth.

Garnet

The deep garnet is associated with the kundalini-fire (or primal-fire) of transformation, which is the integrating fire that assists the kundalini up the spinal column. It is a stone of passion that sometimes needs to be transformed into the power of purity. It is with purity of heart that we are able to see God. In the temple of the human body, the sacred spinal fire lies coiled like a snake and is called the "sacred stone." It is awakened and lifted upward toward the head by the process of transmutation. The sacral plexus is red, but when the fire is lifted toward the mid-section of the body it functions under the blue ray; as it nears the spiritual centers it becomes the purple violet ray.

The red garnets help energize and bring the circulation level to normal if deficient. They also work with the generative system and stimulate the sexual drive. The pink-violet shades work on regeneration and transmutation. All garnets give energy and courage, but beware of passionate love for it can turn into hate because of jealousy. Garnets aid the imagination, and protect against depression and impure thought. They should be worn in cases of rheumatism and arthritis. The garnet lies dormant until it is polished.

Coral

The coral is a gift from our mother ocean to remind us of our eternal foundation. It is actually composed of the skeletons of little animals into reef—plant-like with hard branches. It reminds us of our bones—hard and durable. In shamanic traditions the bones were considered to be the essence of man. Coral teaches us form, also flow and flexibility within form. It lives and breathes in the sea but its roots are anchored in the earth.

It is one of the five sacred stones of the Tibetans and the American Indians. It symbolizes life force energy. It was used as a protection against the evil eye. It has an absorbing quality and turns pale if the wearer is anemic or deficient in blood energy. The darker reds are heating, vitalizing and stimulating to the bloodstream and the entire body. The pink shades have a more direct influence on the heart by restoring harmony where there is a conflict of emotion—as in the water of the subconscious.

Coral is a good aid during meditation or visualization because it helps us retain images and forms. It should be worn in cases of deficient nutrition, depression or lethargy.

Red Jasper

The red jasper is an opaque stone, in which the power of light has not manifested yet. It comes in a variety of colors, combinations and patterns. When polished, it makes a beautiful jewel, reminding us of the colors of the earth. It is a humble and common stone, highly regarded as the mother of all stones, for it carries powerful magical properties. Here is the first transformer, where the earth's energy is changed into human energy. It symbolizes strength, vitality, the physical nature. It adds stimulus that enters the body from the sacral centers and the solar plexus.

Red jasper was highly respected in Peru, and was believed to protect against witchcraft. It sometimes becomes dull in the process of protecting its wearer from negativity or danger because it absorbs vibrations. Because of its qualities, it aids the liver and can help restore the sense of smell.

After working with the stone for a while, I had a dream that jasper relates to having a strong foundation. We must pass through the jasper, and I was reminded that the Pope's ring is jasper—the symbol of the rock, the foundation of the church.

Bloodstone

The bloodstone, sometimes called heliotrope, is a green stone with red flecks of jasper. It has strong healing properties of the physical nature. These "drops of blood" contain much iron and work on the four elements to balance out iron deficiencies in the bloodstream. Together with tourmaline, topaz and carnelian, the bloodstone has the ability to emit directly into the physical body.

It is a good stone for cold weather when people feel cold and have little energy, It invigorates, accelerates and stimulates the whole being.

ORANGE STONES

Carnelian

The carnelian is a symbol of the warm, vitalizing and positive energy of the earth. It reminds us of the work needed here on the planet. Therefore it is a very good grounding and anchoring stone for those inspired beings who need more earth in their nature. We cannot forget, in our spiritual quest, that we are of this planet earth, and that we are needed to do the work here now. We all have the responsibility to aid and uplift in the growth of humanity.

The carnelian has electro-magnetic properties which benefit everyone just by wearing it. It feeds energy directly through the skin, just as we breathe prana by inhaling air. It instills a feeling of well-being and inflowing power. It influences and regulates the intake of food, assimilation, and circulation. It helps keep the digestive system filtered properly.

The best carnelians have a beautiful reddish-gold translucent shine. They can be made into talismans by carving them with universal symbols or letters to create a word, or a prayer for more potency.

The carnelian can become your powerful nature or earth ally. By seeking to connect deeply with the earth, we actually reestablish our connection with the universe.

Fire Opal

The golden-orange fire opal has tremendous power to break up all forms of crystallization in the physical, etheric, or astral body. It has a luminous translucence, which sym-bolizes the fire of sacrifice. It represents our mission of mystical revelation toward illumination. It helps us contact the higher self in order to create less separation between the physical self and the soul self.

The warm orange tints give the positive qualities of vitality, energy, power, and endurance. They aid the digestive system. The deeper reds give energy to the sexual chakra, while the more golden shades influence the solar plexus and the digestive organs. The stone will also help you develop intuition. For more information about the opal, see "White Stones" on page 82.

YELLOW AND GOLD STONES

Topaz

The topaz is an inspiring and stimulating influence on the higher mind and soul. Its golden light reminds us of the halo around the saint's head. It lifts above the mundane, soars up into infinity reaching toward the goal of light. It teaches us the unreality of matter and the eternalness of spirit.

Its electrifying nature magnetizes our whole being, which means that we are charged with a greater capability of awareness, keenness, clarity, concentration and creativity. The electrical charges energize and stimulate, creating voltage throughout the body. This strong influence has a balancing effect on the nervous system and on the solar plexus; (the solar plexus carries anxiety because of conflict and inharmony arising from the body and mind). The topaz is an excellent aid in cases of nervous trauma, exhaustion or mental breakdown.

Amber

Amber is a light-weight gem. Its origin is organic vegetable matter that was composed of various saps. These mineralized and fossilized, sometimes retaining organic inclusions such as insects, ferns and flowers, which give positive additional energies. This wonderful uninterrupted flow of life is a proclamation of the power of nature and the force of electrical charges.

Amber's high vibratory rate purifies and cleans the whole system. It emits a strong magnetic flow, which balances the endocrine and digestive system. This helps to stabilize the spleen, the heart and the base of spine—which in turn helps to open the channels and the correct raising of the serpent fire. The lighter golden stones deal with the mental, while the reddish darker shades deal with the regeneration aspect (or Kundalini energy). They give warmth to cold areas of the body. They reestablish the power of the sun in our own sun center—the solar plexus—which exercises such an important influence on our physical and mental well-being.

Sacred beads were made of amber in the Orient. They were used in meditation and contemplation to help the soul reach enlightenment, to reach the ray of sight or clairvoyance, which gives us external as well as inner vision.

Citrine Quartz

The citrine, through its golden color bears the signature of wisdom and peace. It is a direct stimulant to the mental body and aids in opening the bridge between the higher mental and intuitional levels of the mind. It stimulates cosmic consciousness.

Most of the citrine we see today is amethyst (a violet quartz) which has been baked, turning a golden or reddish yellow. This process resembles a natural process using the power of fire and heat to transform. Of course natural citrine has more power but I believe the baked citrine to carry much potentiality.

The lighter shades promote clarity of thought. They are especially beneficial to the endocrine and digestive systems—cleansing, purifying and eliminating poisons that have accumulated there. The deeper, more fiery shades work upon transmuting fears on an emotional (or mental) level, as well as removing those thought forms from the solar plexus to unblock congestions—even inherited ones. Citrine has the power to calm and soothe disturbed and restless conditions. Its healing influence is of great value against depression, and digestion problems—including constipation and diabetes.

THE PINK STONES

Tourmaline

The tourmaline is an unsurpassable stone, both in benefits and in the beauty of its color. It is very versatile and brings a positive influence to everyone. It does not absorb or hold negativity. It is a sensitive stone for sensitive people. It is subtle, gentle, yet powerful. It is both piezoelectric and pyroelectric. (When pressure is applied to one end of a piezoelectric stone, an electric current flows to the other end. When a stone is termed pyroelectric, it has the ability to produce electric charges when it is heated or cooled. This stone can do both.)

Because of its tremendous electrical nature, the tourmaline influences the nervous system. The nervous system supplies our organs and glands with the vital electricity needed to properly function and maintain balance at all levels of our being. The topaz, amber and carneole all carry this same potent electrical energy.

Tourmaline grows in columns, reminding us of the stalks of plants. It is a gem of translucent light, and sometimes has layers and layers of color—hues and shades of such subtle intensity—that if you are receptive, it will cast a spell of beauty, magic, and fantasy on you. It bestows joy and harmony. From black to clear or colorless, the different shades of this stone will apply to different chakras.

Rubellite or Pink Tourmaline

The rubellite is the queen of the tourmalines. It comes in a solid color variety containing deep red or pink to sometimes violet shades. Its mission is to lead from the heart, strengthening the will to love and to sacrifice. It symbolizes the purity of love that a mother has for her child.

This precious gem aids in directing, channeling and intensifying the devotional urges and impulses within us. It resembles the ruby but is a more subtle balancer of the heart center. It gives insight and perception to emotions, removing conflict and pain that lead us to despair and grief. The rubellite's warm hue helps us open our heart to ourselves, to perceive our own self-worth, our own divinity. Love begins with trusting ourselves, for inside we all have the power to accomplish all things.

Watermelon Tourmaline

The watermelon tourmaline is a bi-colored gem with fascinating qualities. When cross sections are cut, it reminds us of watermelon because of its green rind and pink core.

It symbolizes the pairs of opposites, the principles of yin-yang. Therefore it can help balance and redirect energies. It is great aid in removing imbalances and guilt produced by conflicts and confusion about sexual roles. It teaches us to be self-contained, integrated, secure, and in harmony with our different aspects of self.

This wondrous gem helps us change from being rigid in thought and concept to becoming more open and flexible. It has the capacity to balance conflicting forces outside us and within. It has a great healing and harmonizing influence to the nervous system as well as to the heart. The green part feeds the life force energy into the whole body, while the pink soothes, calms, and harmonizes.

Kunzite

This is a wonderful stone to put near the heart, especially when you use it as a pendant, a brooch, pin, or even wear it in a pouch around your neck. Kunzite grows with a striated structure, resembling the tourmaline—which means that the electrical impulses run the length of the crystal.

This stone relieves old sufferings by acting like a sword of light and truth. It counters pain within the heart. In order to understand how the stone relieves pain, think of the images of Mary or Jesus in which we see swords through their hearts—for kunzite removes pain with a sword-like energy. The deeper shades of color (deeper pink edges) raise the emotions of the heart to a higher level of spirit, so that we can let go of our personal sufferings and face the infinite love of spirit.

The stone comes in many colors: you can use green, blue, or the almost clear version, but my favorite shade is pink.

Rhodochrosite

Rhodochrosite comes in a variety of forms and colors, ranging from bright red crystals to lighter, softer shades of pink, or opaque forms with swirls and patterns. This stone is a good energy conductor and is beneficial to the wearer, for it has a high copper content. It works to integrate physical, mental, and emotional aspects. The pink tones warm and soothe the heart, arousing tender feelings of love, softness, compassion. The orange/pink/red stones are here to teach us love of life, so that we can rejoice about life and share our love with others. The crystal forms that manifest in a golden pink or clear red are of rare beauty and appeal. These stones have a strong influence on the creative process, as well as on the intuitive mind. The clear stones emit a higher frequency than their opaque sisters, although all magnetize and hold force fields around the wearer (or his or her home environment).

The use of pink/gold metal on and around rhodochrosite will amplify its force field. Some gold is more "pink" than other gold, and it is this pink gold that helps make the radiation "soft." Other gems, such as the ruby or amethyst (although serving different purposes), are also augmented by the use of a high copper content in metal, since copper is sometimes mixed with gold when making jewelry. If you set these stones in gold, try to get the "pinkest" gold you can.

Rhodonite

The rhodonite is not as powerful or as beneficial as its sister, rhodochrosite, but is pinkness is an aid to the heart. It comes in light pink shades that are laced with black veins. The black vein in the stone symbolizes the unconscious, while the pink relates to the heart. Using this stone on the heart chakra brings these two aspects of personality together, and the stone promotes peace and quietness where there is mental unrest and confusion.

Rose Quartz

The rose quartz is a strong healer of the heart, especially when you work with the very soft shades of light pink, for the softer shades promote feelings of friendship and good will. It is the stone that all little girls choose when they are given a chance to pick from a whole array of healing stones. This stone is also chosen by many older women who attend healing groups with me. It is humble in its price, and easily affordable as a friendship gift.

GREEN STONES

Emerald

The emerald, a goddess of gems, has the capability to instill divine qualities through the power and beauty of its ray. This golden light, combined with the blue light of infinite spirit, is manifested in the green spark of creativity. The emerald is influenced by Venus and the Moon. It grows profusely in Brazil, Columbia, and Mexico, where it was used in temples and ceremonies. Its beauty inspired the legend of Esmeralda.

It is a symbol of regeneration and life. It represents new birth and the development of a revitalized and beautiful physical body, in which the higher soul will flower with creative and artistic abilities.

The emerald is soothing and sympathetic, giving peace and harmony to the body, heart, soul and spirit. This ray of nature also carries the power to align us with natural forces. It is both energizing and restful, replenishing and calming. Its powerful clear ray magnetizes and amplifies, focuses and directs its light, much like a laser beam, transmuting illness.

It emits vibrations of balance, healing and infinite patience to all who need attunement and inspiration, providing us with a serene inner lift. The force field of the emerald is effective, whether in its natural raw state, or when faceted—except for the more opaque variety (which is better used in the treatment of physical, rather than emotional ailments). The clear shades of the emerald are good for meditation, inspiration, and healing.

In Egypt and in the orient the emerald is believed to have wonderful curative properties for the eyes and was worn to protect against the evil eye. Lapidaries sometimes refresh their eyes with emerald water.

It is a symbol of abundance and richness. Therefore to bring these properties into your life, I recommend that everyone drink emerald water for three or seven days. Put the emerald in a glass of water, let it stand overnight, remove the stone in the morning, then drink making an affirmation and giving thanks. It is the essence of the stone you are drinking—much like taking flower-remedies in which the essence works on the etheric body.

Please wear the emerald alone or with a diamond, which represents the white light. If it is worn with other stones its power is decreased or nullified.

Malachite

Malachite is a symbol of creativity and change. The marvelous patterns of eyes, spirals, circles alternating with shaded bands indicate that the stone is a symbol of change. Malachite gives us the message of the green fire in the black void of the unfolding universe. Its density and opaqueness represent the physical—the material. We must overcome density if we are to endure on this planet. Through the process of creating with material expression, we come to understand the nature of spirit. Malachite's essence of alterability touches all parts of our bodies and souls.

The malachite was the sacred stone of the ancient Egyptians, who used the stone in several different ways. It was worn on the body for protection and for safeguarding pregnancy. The stones were laid on the body, as I do today, for healing and balancing and harmonizing the whole system. They were ground in a paste and used as an eye remedy, as well as a cosmetic. Malachite heals the physical body as well as the inner eye, the heart, the total being.

I would like to share a personal experience that happened a few years ago. A friend and I walked up to a dried up river bed in the desert of Arizona. We had taken many pieces of malachite with us on our walk. After giving thanks to our stones, we laid them on our bodies—over the chakras and our faces. We then traveled on a strange and magical journey. My body went through a powerful healing, and my spirit flew over the desert, along with the eagle and the hawk. I looked down and understood the earth. A rebirth, a regeneration of the body, soul and spirit had taken place! Since that time I have loved and trusted this most powerful stone. It has become my most healing ally.

Jade

Jade is the most respected stone in the Orient, where it has been a symbol of peace and tranquility because of its marvelous calming attributes. It has a subtle impact, which works over a long period of time to raise consciousness in everyone. It doesn't absorb negative influences, but constantly emits the healing vibration of harmony. Jade, and members of its family (nephrite and jadeite), come in many lovely hues. The light white or cream shades are soothing to the general nervous system. The pale mauves and lilacs relate to the heart center, balancing and calming the emotions. The deeper greens and the imperial greens are overall balancers and healers of the entire being.

Jade instills feelings of sacrifice that relate to emotional growth. In ancient China, the "Jade Emperor" was a cosmic deity associated with power in the service of sacrifice. He also represented the giving and sustaining of the following virtues over a lifetime: humility, wisdom, justice, and courage.

In Mexico, as well as in Eastern countries, exquisite carvings were made of jade because it was a strong stone. In China, jade carvings of dragons had a double meaning of protection and inner strength, good luck and long life. In China many wore several jade pendants from a belt, for the jade brought protection, and the jade pieces hitting each other made a wonderful sound when one walked.

The message of harmony from this stone is universal. As Confucius once said:

> ...Wise men have seen in jade all the different virtues. It is soft, smooth, and shining—like kindness; it is hard, fine, and strong—like intelligence; its edges seem sharp, but do not cut like justice; it hangs down to the ground—like humility; when struck, it gives a ringing sound—like music; the stains in it which are not hidden, and which add to its beauty—are like truthfulness; its brightness is like heaven, and its fine substance

(born of the mountains and water) is like the earth.*

Green Tourmaline

The green tourmaline comes in a variety of shades providing us with the balancing power of nature. It is subtle yet dynamic. It quiets the mind via the nervous system, creating in us the will to achieve widsom and ease conflicts.

It is serene, restorative, and healing with the potential of rejuvenating and regenerating our entire body. It realigns our mental bodies by shattering old concepts and pushing us to begin anew on a different level of consciousness.

Each one of us is guided to the right shade needed. The green tourmaline is a great healer of illnesses of the heart, problems with blood pressure, or for asthmatic conditions.

Green and Colorless Tourmaline

This is a bi-colored gem that has the quality of calming and balancing the brain and nerve fluids. Its soothing vibration is a great aid in healing headaches and inflammation.

Chrysoprase

The chrysoprase, an apple-green translucent gem, is an excellent balancer of both the physical and mental body. It steadily emits a serene flow of light, which has a sedative and tranquilizing effect on the wearer. It seems to clarify problems, bringing unconscious thoughts to a conscious level, as well as helping develop a higher consciousness and strengthening inner vision.

---

*author's translation

The chrysoprase is a great healing influence, creating more balance and purpose for those who have neurotic patterns of behavior. The darker green shades have a more powerful frequency than the lighter shades. However, all can be used as tools for quieting the disturbances that relate to inferiority or superiority complexes, and it also works for mild hysteria. Its golden green light is also effective in feeding, recharging, and calming the heart.

Peridot

The peridot has a golden-green soft glow. Because of its high content of yellow within the green, it has the quality of developing our mental capabilities, as well as supplying balance and tranquility to the emotions. It was used by the Atlanteans, Egyptians, Aztecs, Incas and Toltecs as a calming, purifying and balancing energy for the physical body.

Peridot has very cleansing effects. It is of great value in the digestion of food, relieving constipation, helping ulcerous and inflamed conditions of the bowel, and restoring energy to the spleen. This stone of the sun helps us open inner sight, relieving melancholia and giving inspiration.

Dioptase

Dioptase, with its beautiful, deep green crystals, is a young stone evolving into the vibrational potency of emeralds. Its strong healing green light reminds us of abundance and earth. Not much is known yet about this gem, but I am personally very pulled to it. Its beauteous green light is inspiring. I wear a ring that has one large deep green crystal, which reminds me of the green dragon light of protection and life, good fortune and strength. Try it to see what it does for you.

Aventurine

This is a fairly translucent quartz with a little glitter. It does not carry powerful healing vibrations but is an excellent touchstone, bringing calmness and serenity. It is very good to keep around yourself in your home.

Moss Agate

The moss agate comes in different shades of green and has the appearance of moss, which reminds us of growing plants. It is not so much a healer—but it carries the energy of nature and is an aid to all who work the land. It can be used as a touchstone.

Green Jasper

The green jasper is a stone with a strong earth feeling, useful around your home. Its frequency is beneficial in balancing those who are drawn to it. Its influence is calming.

BLUE/GREEN STONES

Aquamarine

The aquamarine, a transparent luminous gem, is the stone of mystics and pure-souled seers who feel everything. The green blue of the cosmic sea reflects the light effects of the sun on waves. Its effect is subtle and soft, yet long-lasting, touching our spirit in a deep way.

It has a great balancing effect on all levels, stabilizing the emotional, mental and physical bodies. It is an excellent purifier and I use its wonderful properties to clear the throat of impure thoughts that are congested there. The aquamarine helps us retain purity and innocence while helping us achieve clarity of vision. It helps against nerve pains, gland troubles, disorders of the neck, jaw, throat, and toothache.

Turquoise

The turquoise is a symbol of the blue of the sea and the sky. Infinity in the ocean speaks of the depth of the soul. Infinity in the sky speaks of the limitless heights of ascension. The stone is opaque as the earth, yet it lifts the spirit high, giving us wisdom of both earth and sky. It is old, yet young.

The turquoise has been held as a most sacred stone by ancient and contemporary cultures who are mystically and spiritually inclined. The symbolism of its color has led to the belief that we are of the spirit. It was sacred in Egypt along with malachite and lapis lazuli. It was sacred to the Persian culture, where it symbolized purity. It is highly respected by Tibetan Buddhists and the American Indian, for they believe that it holds the atmosphere surrounding the earth and sky, giving life and breath. American Indians believe it to be a protector and guardian of the body and soul. Both cultures combine it with coral for polarity (earth—red, and spirit— blue). The stone was worn in the navel by gypsies, who feel it is good for everything. The combination is shown in Plate 1 on page 87.

In Tibet there is a bridge called the turquoise bridge. Prayer wheels and charm boxes are usually decorated with turquoise because it is believed to bring good fortune. The stone is mounted on rings and worn in the hair. Tibetan women used to wear large hairpieces covered with turquoise stones, to display their hair to maximum advantage.

The turquoise has the capacity to absorb negative feelings that would have come to its wearer. Its color changes when the wearer is ill, or when something unpleasant is about to happen. Sometimes it cracks in the service of protection and sacrifice. The stone carries a strong healing vibration, which is magnified by its high copper content.

Chrysocolla

The chrysocolla is a younger sister of the turquoise. Although the symbology of the two stones is very similar, chrysocolla is moving into a higher sphere of consciousness. A stone of Venus, it is a symbol of beauty, love, and harmony. It is gentle but powerful. It does resemble the turquoise, but the chrysocolla carries more light.

The chrysocolla aids in balancing and calming the emotions, bringing peace to the heart and mind. It helps to alleviate fears and guilt that prevent us from relaxing. The stone can help restore harmony. It is a soft stone, and because it is easy to grind, it can be used in the preparation of remedies.

BLUE STONES

Sapphire

The sapphire's power lies in the rays it emits, the color of the sky, the blue light of the heavens. It has the highest light of all blue stones. This gem, matter from earth, transformed by the blue ray, spiritualizes, cleanses and heals.

Its deep, penetrating light emits rays of pure devotion, which speak to us of cosmic infinity, higher mystery, and infinite reality. It has the power to transform, to lift our soul into higher realms. The sapphire has been used in the performance of higher mysteries. Its sacred beauty inspired religious devotion, inner devotion and faith. It is a great meditation tool which has been used by yogis, healers and saints.

The blue sapphire is very healing on the throat center, which is the center of purity, where thoughts and words must be cleansed. The throat is the gateway to the spiritual aspect of our being, our devotional and mystical nature. It is the passage that connects our heart to our thinking process. It is there that most of us have blocks. Because of old repressions, which were not expressed with words, congestions were created. In order to manifest our true intentions we must have an open flow in that area. The throat chakra is our contact with the universe, and very important in developing our consciousness, our thoughts.

The sapphire is manifested in a variety of blue shades from light to deep indigo. The lighter shades create a mood of serene optimism and are good for meditation. The indigo sapphire is discussed under Indigo Stones.

The star sapphire group is not as powerful but aids in creating and manifesting thoughts of devotion. This gem is illumined with a point of light caused during the cutting. The clear or colorless sapphire filters thoughts. The yellow sapphire cleans impure thoughts.

Lapis Lazuli

Lapis lazuli has an opaque light of deep royal blue, which is symbolic of the vastness of the infinite spirit of the heavens. It has been a sacred stone of ancient cultures such as Atlantis, Egypt, the East, and Mexico. It is a symbol of the illumination of the mind, and as such, has a great history. In Egypt, scarabs were carved from it to doubly signify infinity, as the animal and the stone are both symbolic of infinity. Esoteric knowlege was sometimes inscribed on this stone in the form of a talisman or amulet.

The stone is very important in the foundation of the earth, as it represents absolute light. It touches at the very heart of love and beauty, harmonizing the inner as well as the outer. Lapis lazuli instills high idealism by reaching to build and establish the essence of fellowship and cooperation.

This is a gem of contemplation and meditation, inspiring us toward our eternal soul so we may know that love, immortality and God are one. Stones of deep luminosity, with bright exotic hues of blue are the most useful. The pyrite inclusions—the gold flecks that show that it is genuine lapis—give it a shine and an unusually positive energy.

Lapis has great healing, curative, and purifying properties when used on the body. Its deep blue rays penetrate knots and congested areas of the throat, releasing them and opening the passage for the sacred word. What has been said about the throat in the section about the blue sapphire also applies here, but on a more physical level because of the opaqueness of the stone. We need to release thoughts and emotions that prevent us from expressing the true self. Speech is our highest attribute, and the modulations of the voice are indicative of our evolutionary development. Its cooling ray is also a great aid in swellings and inflammations. It is interesting to note the law of opposition here—when something burns red, we need to apply a cooling blue.

Blue Topaz

The blue topaz is a beautiful, brilliant, translucent gem. Its electric light blue ray is cooling, calming and inspiring. (See Golden Topaz for more information.)

Its magic lies in the powerful properties of magnetism, which transmit and receive much like tourmaline and amber. Its message of eternity, in addition to the electrical power contained within, makes it a very powerful stone of radiant light, clarity, purity and spiritual seeking. It is a great cleanser and purifier which can be used on the throat and for the nerves.

The blue topaz could be of great benefit to creative artists for they could use it to imbue themselves with the inspiration of its rays before beginning a new work.

Sodalite

Sodalite is a deep blue stone still in a process of evolution. It resembles lapis lazuli, but on a lower level of function. It is too dense to be considered a meditative or reflective stone. It has been used as jewelry and is also carved into objects.

Its power can be amplified when used in conjunction with another gem of the same blue vibration. It aids in balancing the glands that control our metabolism. Because this stone is reasonably priced, you may wish to use it to work on the throat chakra as a "helper" to the more expensive lapis lazuli.

INDIGO STONES

Indigo Sapphire

The indigo sapphire has an illuminating quality for it enhances all activities of the wisdom manifestation. Its keynote is universality: God in Man, Man in God. The power of its ray develops our intuitive and clairvoyant perceptions so we may more clearly see the light of truth and thus reach wisdom. It sweeps all confusion and illusion away from the intellect, bringing reason to the seeking soul. It teaches us to differentiate between illusion and knowledge.

The indigo sapphire works on transfiguring different aspects of mind, bridging the gap between concrete thought and abstract concepts. It is ruled by Saturn, which in the future will no longer be considered the planet of obstruction as it is today, but will be looked upon as the pathfinder for the illumined.

It has great healing value in the treatment of mental disorders, where it is able to expel negative elements in the consciousness and build up higher ones.

Azurite

Azurite is a crystalline gem of deep blue with a touch of purple, reminding us of the "eye of the spirit." It is a symbol of inner knowledge and wisdom. It represents high sensitivity, spiritual perception, true occultism, intuition, and clairvoyance. This stone has enormous potential in helping to unlock the gate to heaven because of the power of vision it bestows upon us. Its nature is beyond thought and emotion; it is another dimension of experience—of being.

It is a wonderful stone to put on the third eye during a meditation, because it projects spiritual vision to the differing perceptions of ultimate truths or cosmic awareness. It opens us to the "inner seeing" and removes the blocks there. It is a great healer of human development, and is not particularly good as a stone for jewelry.

The azurite is a stone that can be used by students who are studying for exams. It helps open the mind so that it is more receptive, helping students retain information. Put it on your desk or near where you are studying.

VIOLET STONES

Amethyst Quartz

The amethyst is a symbol of transmutation, indicating an alchemical process of the physical, emotional, and spiritual nature. It occurs in both crystalline and non-crystalline forms in varying hues of violet. The color is usually deepest on the top of the crystal.

This gem relates to the crown of the head (the crown chakra), which is the sanctuary of the spirit, the gateway for higher forces. The lower red fire of sensual life has been lifted to the pure blue of the spiritual. Red of activity is blended with blue of divinity. Purple has been a symbol of majesty, a spiritualized nature made noble by sorrow. When the lower nature is purified, one is worthy of the "purple robe," the ultimate goal at the end of the path.

The amethyst works on many levels and aspects of our being—at the edges and borders of our perceptions—where the mysteries are held. It is a gem of inspiration, which encourages meditation and the love of God, calling us to a selfless giving and service to humanity. Its spirituality was recognized by the early Christians who chose it as a symbol of self-sacrifice, purity, and chastity—all virtues of the Piscean Age.

The amethyst is an energizer that has the potential to transmute consciousness, transforming set patterns and habits that relate to ideas and emotions. It dispels anger and rage, fear and anxiety, which block our spirits from realizing realms of infinity. It clarifies our dreams.

The stone can be of great use in healing, especially in conjunction with color therapy (which uses the projection of violet light), augmenting the value of the gem crystal itself. Because of the ultraviolet spectrum contained within, it is of great use in the molecular and cellular alteration of organic substances, be they plant, animal or human. Also, because of the ultraviolet spectrum, it works along with ultrasonic wavelengths of sound in the fields of music therapy, medical surgery, and even on levels we are unable to see.

Because the amethyst has such a high density vibration, it is potent for all forms of severe pain. It helps physical pain as well as the pain caused by suffering and sorrow. It even helps those who are psychologically ill, bringing comfort and relief. Amethyst is a great help in headaches and cases of insomnia. When working with headaches or insomnia, poke and rub the temples of your head gently with the top and the side of the stone. Its vibration is also effective in treating diseases arising from impurities of the blood, such as eczema, boils, and even venereal diseases.

The deepest shades of the stone, which are the most powerful transformers, work with the kundalini energy balancing and stabilizing problems of sexual polarity and differentiation. The deeper blue shades were used in religious ceremonies, and work at diffusing and removing old habit patterns. The lightest shades (mauve and lavender) are very inspiring to the mystically inclined, or to students of the occult arts, giving a serene brilliance to the aura. The shades of lilac symbolize outreaching love for humanity. Orchid shades symbolize the idealism that belongs to the New Age.

At this time, there is a great deal of amethyst growing in the earth because our mother planet needs to realign and rebalance herself. All of us can afford to purchase this stone, for it is quite inexpensive, especially when you consider its beauty and the help it provides us.

Always remember that a balance of both body (red) and spirit (blue) needs to take place, so we may merge with the cosmos and be one with the infinite divine.

Fluorite

Fluorite is a young gem that is still evolving into its full potential. Its crystals are cubic-like forms in a variety of exquisite hues that range from pale lavender to a deep bluish purple. The stone is a catalyst of transmutation which can lead to inspirational devotion, cosmic truth and wisdom. As we learn to love the infinite in all, we will find joy in all.

The fluorite's message states that wisdom comes from harmony, that harmony comes from contemplation, that contemplation comes from peace, that inner peace leads to inner light and inner gladness. This gem has healing potential that resembles the amethyst. It aids in mental disorders and spiritual awakenings.

Some fluorites are shades of green, and the green stones are a great help at grounding excess energies. They help us operate at optimum efficiency, even while handling tremendous amounts of frequencies in our own physical body. Some fluorites (octohedrons) contain many colors of the rainbow. If you find such a stone, it can be used on the third eye, as well as to enhance meditation and relaxation.

WHITE STONES

Moonstone

The moonstone is an ancient gem of important spiritual significance. It is connected to the moon and the female aspect of our emotional nature. It is a great help in cooling, calming and soothing overreactions to emotional and personal situations.

It was a sacred stone to the culture of India, where the carvings of temple doors were adorned with moonstones, depicting male-female embraces. These symbolized the oneness of our dual aspects and integrated the emotional and dream nature of our being.

The moonstone is a stone of inner growth and strength, assisting our soul in its progress. At the time of a full moon or menstruation, women need to be careful of their super sensitive emotional nature and remove these stones. Too much of anything is not beneficial.

It comes in almost transparent white color, sometimes with a blue light and in warmer tones of cream. The clear, finely polished ones serve best.

I recommend the moonstone to men, to help them open their feminine or emotional side, and many friends have asked that I get this stone for their sons.

Opal

The opal is a slightly translucent and mysterious stone, in which the spectrum of colors from milky white to black is represented—reflecting totality. These flashes of opalescent color and fire can be utilized to reach the highest spiritual levels of inner sight. The iridescent colors of the rainbow work on all the chakras. Some opals are able to work on more than one center at a time, equalizing and balancing as necessary.

The entire opal family lifts ordinary consciousness to cosmic awareness so we may feel more united in our inner being, lessening the gap between the physical and the soul.

The opal is a very porous stone that can crack and shatter easily. The reflection and refraction of light on the water combined in the stone and tiny cracks of the opal cause the opalescent quality in the shifting colors. The milky, opaque and shimmering variety serves in soothing the emotional nature. The color predominant in other opals works on the related chakra.

It has been considered an unlucky stone at certain times because it absorbs the nagativity of an individual and then returns it. This follows the Law of Return, or Karma, which means that our thoughts need to be purified before wearing the stone or we shall be confronted with our own negativity.

It is the gem that best demonstrates that stones jump, disappear, or hide from the wearer. If it is not suited to an individual at a particular time, it will not be found. When the time is right it will reappear.

The opal should not be worn with other stones.

Pearl

The pearl is the jewel of the sea, and is found in the shells of oysters. The grain of sand, or other irritant, which is the causative seed in the development of the pearl gives us the message of transmutation.

We can compare the pearl to our own development, our own struggle for inner growth, and realize that no matter how humble or oppressed, we can all attain the incredible beauty of a pearl. The message of the pearl is to show us that we can become inwardly free by shattering mental and emotional patterns—we can change and grow beautiful.

The pearl absorbs negative energy from the wearer and boomerangs the energy back, and although it may appear to be a painful process, the pearl actually aids the wearer when he or she needs to deal with self-confrontation.

Naturally sea-grown pearls are more powerful than cultured pearls, and it is a good idea to try to obtain the pearls that have grown naturally if you can. The lustre varies depending on the temperature of the sea water the pearl grew in. The variety known as the "baroque pearl" manifest when it has stayed too long in the shell and has lost its roundness. When pearls get dull, a good way to refresh their lustre is to dip them into their natural home—sea water.

Never mix pearls with other stones, especially the diamond, as any conflicts of self would be greatly magnified, and the combination could create a great deal of disharmony. If you are drawn to the pearl, it may mean that a purification through self-confrontation is of important value to you.

The pearl has curative powers because of the calcium, mineral, and protein content from its original source.

BLACK STONES

Black Tourmaline

The black tourmaline is a symbol of the mysterious—that which is unperceived and unseen—the abstract. The sleekness of the black crystals reminds us that life essence must have form in order to manifest and become visible.

Black tourmaline is the most beneficial of all black stones because of its power and quality as an electrical transformer. It handles negativity by deflection rather than absorption, as most other black gems do. It becomes a protective shield to all those who are susceptible to negative energies. This creates a whole different concept about wearing a black gem.

The stone instills seriousness, self-control, discipline and great staying power. It helps to clarify abstract thoughts and concepts.

Black Obsidian

The black obsidian, as all black stones, belongs to Saturn. It teaches us that through pain and sorrow, the ego is lifted above the trivial and its attention is focused upon the spirit. It is a stabilizer and chastener. Regeneration and illumination often follow sickness and grief, for experiences that cause sickness and grief are the ego's supreme teacher.

The obsidian is a glass-like volcanic stone, which is sometimes gleaming black (as the stone from Demlos in Greece), or it may be flecked with white spots. This stone has been used in ceremonies by certain American Indian tribes, because it is believed to sharpen outer and inner vision. Its sharpness was used in the making of knives, spearheads, arrowheads and needles.

Jet

Jet is a shiny black stone and carries the same qualities as black obsidian. It is a soft stone that has been often used in jewelry and carvings. Jet is actually a carbon that is very old and highly compressed.

The stone is associated with mourning, and carries certain negative energies of the past, such as black coral, which was misused in black magic. Black jet knives were used in sacrificial ceremonies at Stonehenge. However, in Ireland, where the sea is turbulent, the Irish fisherman's wife burns a small piece of jet while praying for her husband's safe return from the sea.

Powdered jet was used around an aching tooth, to cure it, before there were dentists. It has also been used to cure stomach ache and headache.

Plate 1. An arrangement of coral and turquoise symbolizing the earth and the sky.

Plate 2. Some of the crystals and stones that I use for healing and meditation.

Plate 3. An arrangement of different forms, colors, and hues of quartz crystals.

Plate 4. A mandala of stones indicating the seven rays of the rainbow. See figure 2 on page 54 for more discussion of how to make a mandala like this for yourself.

Plate 5. Red jasper, upper left; fire opal, upper right; golden topaz, lower left; carnelian, lower right. All these stones give warmth.

Plate 6. A grouping of various golden stones in the upper left; amber, upper right; rhodolite, lower left; emerald, lower right.

Plate 7. Malachite, upper left; jade, upper right; green tourmaline, lower left; green/colorless tourmaline, lower right.

Plate 8. Dioptase, upper left; turquoise, upper right; moonstone, lower left; amethyst, lower right.

Plate 9. The healer holds blue gemstones just before they will be put on the throat chakra, face, and brow (the third eye). They will bring calm, release tension and blocks from the throat and face, as well as opening the third eye.

Plate 10. Here a patient is holding the stones in her hand. By holding the crystals like this, she is able to receive energy, strength, and the calming properties of the crystal. This technique also allows excess energies to pass through and out of her body through the fingers.

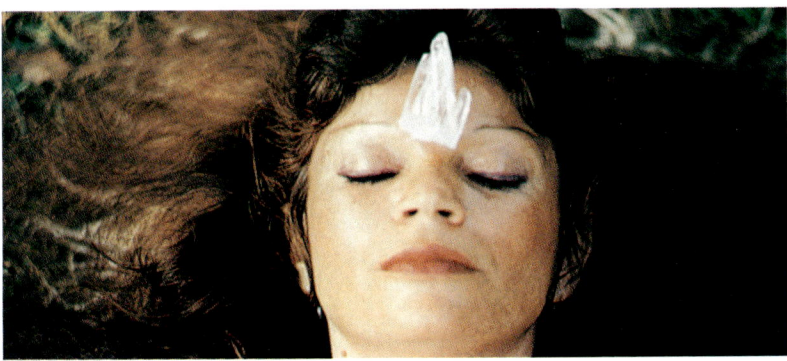

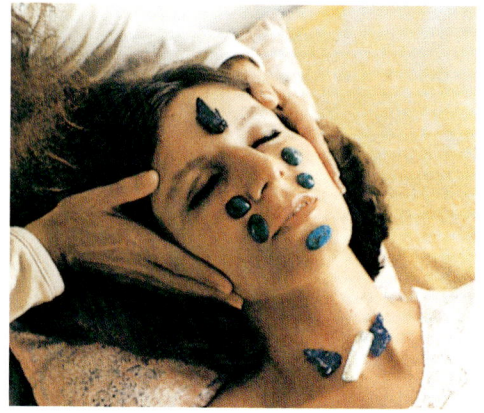

Plate 12. Lapis lazuli and aquamarine are on the throat chakra to release blocks so that emotions may be expressed. The turquoise on the face brings calmness and harmony to areas of tension. An azurite crystal on the brow lets the third eye (the sixth chakra) recognize truth and wisdom.

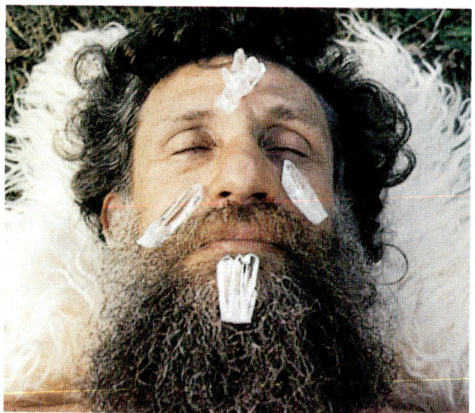

Plate 13. Here quartz crystals are being used to rebalance the energies of the face, bringing a sense of well-being and bringing more light and clarification to the third eye.

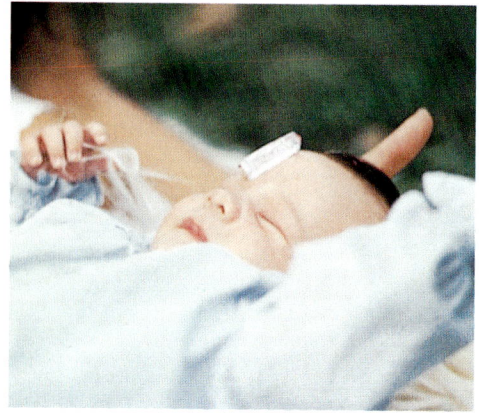

Plate 14. This baby was calmed and soothed by the crystal.

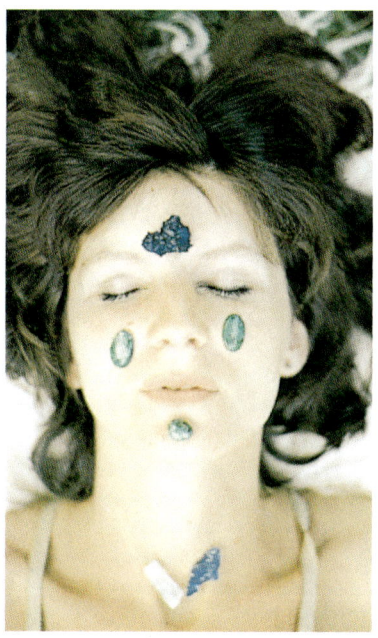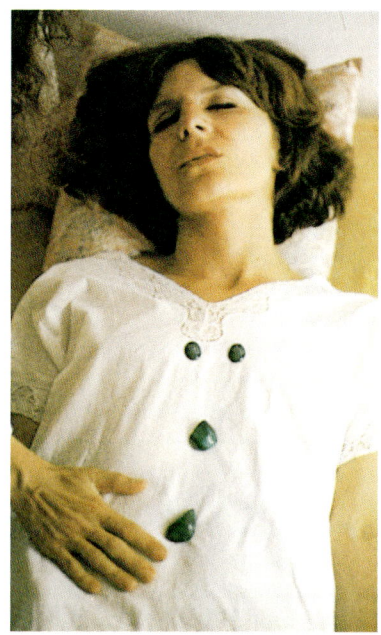

Plate 15. Left: An azurite sits on the third eye (the sixth chakra) to open the inner eye to higher dimensions of truth. This woman felt a great deal of pain and suffering in her heart chakra, and nervousness and anxiety came from the solar plexus (third chakra). She was a young woman when she came to me, and memories of childhood losses were being confronted during this healing. Right: Here I have used malachite to bring balance and harmony to the nervous system.

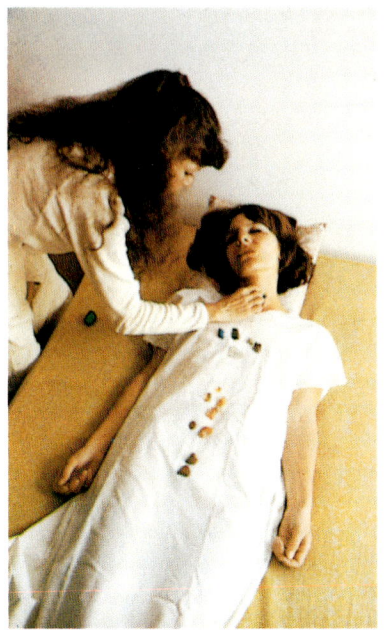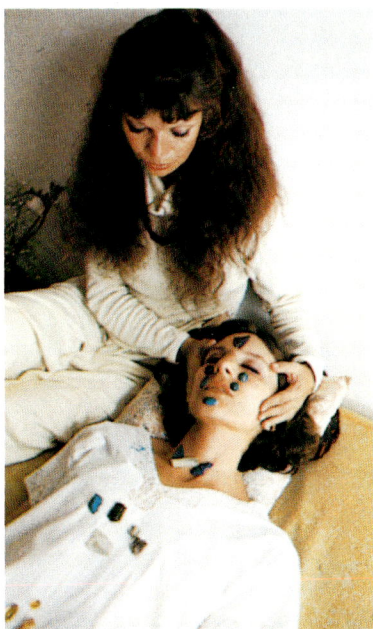

Plate 16. This is a very simple layout of stones for quieting, calming, harmonizing, and bringing a sense of well-being to the total self. The stones are used in the rainbow method: red, orange, gold, pink and green, blue, turquoise, indigo. I have put turquoise and chrysocolla on the face to release tension and bring harmony. When the stones bring inner harmony, the woman can begin to heal herself. On the left I am laying the stones on the throat chakra. On the right, I am sitting with the patient while the stones are working.

7 Healing Magic

NATURE OF DISEASE

We need to understand the nature of disease, for illness is caused mostly by old patterns, by reactions to actions and deeds, by fears, or by overindulgence—which is usually a sign of anxieties and conflicts. These conflicts between soul and personality create imbalance and disharmony in the body. The most important phase of healing is the awakening realization that by understanding the cause, we can cure and heal ourselves.

The subconscious mind is so old, and so deeply rooted in our being—so primitive—it is difficult for us to understand its full power. It is the creative force within each of us that manifests whatever the conscious mind impresses on it. Therefore, to achieve true and lasting healing, we must become aware of our thoughts and actions. We must go deeply into ourselves and examine those emotions, patterns, and images that our minds have created. It is not easy to do this, and many people settle for treating only the symptoms of disease.

Today, the modern American Indian goes to a regular doctor to treat the symptoms of the illness in his body. But he goes to a shaman to find the cause so he can treat his spirit. Perhaps we need to learn to do this, too.

HEALTH IS HARMONY

In this chapter, we will focus on the use of crystals and stones for healing and re-establishing harmony and balance in the entire being. The power of the stones comes from the earth and the cosmos. Their beauty is a result of their perfected qualities.

We are now living in an era of great cleansing and purifying for everyone. It is often painful and uncomfortable to experience this change. The crystals and stones are the catalysts that bring about the purification. The soul, in its own process of growth and development, calls for this realignment with the cosmos.

The New Age fundamentally signifies a change in consciousness—we are moving from an era of isolation and separation to one of attunement and communion. The isolation has caused a great deal of conflict, grief, sorrow and suffering. Let us accept the oneness of everything so we can return to our roots and find our meaning.

The healing process on this planet begins with each individual. We must have the courage to keep seeking into the nature of life, to reach insights into the nature of Self, to look into our own hearts and souls so we can fight the evil there. "To thine own self be true."

IMPORTANCE OF BREATH

Deep rhythmic breathing is of great value. It enables us to draw in a much greater supply of prana (or energy) from the air and sun. Therefore it is important that we check our breathing regularly, and practice deep breathing on a regular basis.

Color breathing techniques can be used to energize the total being. These act as a tonic for tired nerves and minds. One mentally visualizes the life-giving radiance of the color ray. Each of the seven rays may be breathed according to a specific need.

The first three rays—red, orange and yellow—are magnetic and should be visualized as flowing up from the earth toward the solar plexus (the third chakra). The last three rays—blue, indigo, and violet—are electrical and should be breathed from the ether downward. The green ray is the balancing ray for the spectrum, and it flows in the system horizontally.

It is thought that we are now living in the period ruled by the fourth (or green) ray, which is the midpoint between the lower periods of soul growth and the higher spiritual awakening. It is time for all of us to open our heart centers to learn the meaning of universal love.

MEDITATIONS FOR HEALING AND HARMONIZING

Find yourself a quiet place, put a stone of the color needed in front of you, and immerse yourself in that ray. The stone's vibrations can initiate spiritual growth and unfoldment if you are genuinely receptive. Practice the following system using mental affirmations. Thoughts are viatal and creative, so think good and true things for yourself. Practice good intentions.

There is a correlation between the chakras and the color rays. The first chakra is red, the second orange, the third yellow, the fourth green, the fifth blue, the sixth indigo, and the seventh chakra is violet. As you begin using the chakras and colors, you may use any of the following meditations:

1. To obtain health, vitality, or energy—use rose-red or orange.

2. For rebuilding health after illness—tune yourself to green, blue and violet. Change your thoughts to cheerful radiant thoughts of ease, health, and peace.

3. For depression, loneliness or frustration—use the seven rays. Yellow is one of the most powerful forces against depression or limitations of any kind.

4. For prosperity, success, or progress—green is the great source of universal supply. This vibration will attract the things you want. It is the ray that enriches the personality and raises the vibrations of success and abundance.

5. For mental development and mind power—use the golden ray that emanates from the infinite center of wisdom, for it provides greater mental efficiency and illumination.

6. For total protection and filling the whole body with cosmic energy, health, and peaceful vibrations—use the white light.

7. To comprehend the nature of the dream state— use black. It also helps to gain mental understanding when you are too nervous or cannot concentrate.

LAYING THE STONES ON THE BODY

There are several ways to practice treatments with the stones. You may wish to try any or all of the methods listed here as you begin to practice. And the more you practice working with the stones, the better you will become!

1. Using only quartz crystal, put the crystals on all the chakras for an overall balancing and harmonizing treatment. This will shift all the energies in the body. The clear quartz crystals are excellent absorbers of negativity, and they perform the

unique service of removing negativity from, around, or in the body—or even from a room or an area. Crystal aids in balancing the aura by decongesting the various force centers (or chakras) that get blocked in all of us from time to time. You can also massage with the crystal. This has been discussed in Chapter 4 on page 35. Remove the crystals in twenty to thirty minutes.

2. Lay only green stones on all the chakras for an overall nourishing, or harmonizing of the total being. Malachite is an excellent stone for this. Remove the stones after twenty to thirty minutes have passed.

3. Lay the various stones that correlate with the chakras on the appropriate chakra. Here the stones act as catalysts. They are receptors and transmitters of light. Except for a few stones, such as malachite, lapis lazuli and jasper, one can say that the more light in the stone, the more healing power the stone possesses. I will discuss the procedure of this treatment in more detail later in the chapter. Again, when laying the stones on the chakras, remove them after twenty to thirty minutes.

OTHER HEALING USES OF STONES

Centuries and centuries ago, long before the age of aspirin, the ancients used *touchstones*. Magic makers and adepts could cure humanity of various nervous and mental ills this way. They could bring tranquility into people's homes. In China, Tibet, the holy temples of India, and the great temples of the Aztecs, Incas, and Mayans, the priests laboriously shaped these stones by hand. It is said that the stones had contours that comforted the human brain by providing pleasant sensations that calmed the system. In some cultures, touch beads serve the same purpose and some people still use "worry beads." Touchstones not only calm us, they ground us by reminding us to touch the core in ourselves. The stone acts as a mirror of the self.

Ancient remedies used *powdered* (or pulverized) *stones* for treating ailments. For example, amber was used to treat problems with kidneys, liver or constipation. Powdered amber was ground into a flour, then mixed with honey and a little water, and swallowed. Malachite was used in a paste form to cure cataracts. It was applied to the eyes. Elixirs, tinctures and some homeopathic pellets are composed of stones—such as lapis lazuli or turquoise. I don't suggest that anyone experiment with these remedies unless they have attained the proper medical qualifications to do so.

Magnetized water was quite popular, and we still use it today. Certain gems (such as an emerald, ruby, diamond or quartz crystal) can be used for simple water remedies. Magnetized water is made by putting the chosen stone into a glass of water for several hours (or overnight), charging the water with the special energy of the stone. You may put the water in the sun for extra power, but only if you are in a clean and natural environment. The essence is important. This essence (used, for example, in the Bach flower remedies) of the stone affects the entire body. You may want to try one of the following experiments:

1. To bring abundance and health, drink emerald water. Please refer to Chapter 6, page 68, for additional information.

2. For purification and lifting the heart, as well as for intestinal pains, drink ruby water.

3. For overall healing, protection and illumination, drink the water from a diamond or from a quartz crystal.

You can also use *solarized power*. The properties of the life-giving energies of the sun can be used to rebuild health. The Egyptians used bowls encrusted with gems of the same color as the juices of certain foods put in them. These were put out into the sunlight to become charged with the energy of Ra. Sometimes the bowls were made with stones such as agate, lapis lazuli, malachite, or jasper. Today, we can follow the same principle, by putting our stones in the sunlight for recharging. (See also the section that discusses cleansing your stones, page 30.)

INTERCONNECTION IN HEALING

It is important to know that an interconnection takes place between the healer, the patient, and the stones whenever healing takes place. True healing is a partnership between all three. Contact and rapport are established between the healer and the patient when both have let go of the personality barrier (or social graces, if you prefer that term). This allows the patient to let the power flow out. A partnership of harmony and cooperation is the aim. The more open and receptive they both are, the stronger the results. It is the very element of trust and acceptance that makes a treatment successful. The reactions that I have witnessed over the years have left no doubt in my mind that the crystals and stones are very powerful.

It is this faith and belief in the crystals and stones which gives me strength as a transmitter or channel for healing. The stones carry the beautiful and purposeful mission of alleviating disease and pain—not with drugs—but with the radiant power of light which works on all levels of our being. We suffer because we are unable to illumine our lives.

It is a magical and marvelous experience to see the radiant stones on the body. You can watch them fulfilling their purpose, for they do their work by shifting energies and unblocking congested areas, they release pain trapped in the different centers (such as the heart and throat chakras), and they calm the anxiety and fear in the solar plexus.

PROCEDURE FOR HEALING WITH STONES

In order to work with the stones, it is best to make sure that your patient is comfortable. Some peole come in wearing very tight or uncomfortable clothing, or colors and fabrics that I don't care for. So I ask that everyone change (in another room) into a loose garment of white. I have made my own, but you can buy white robe-like garments made of cotton, that you can easily wash and take care of. The garment should close, so a large size white dress, or large men's shirts, would work well.

The patient and I first come together in a breath meditation. This means that we do several kinds of breathing before starting the healing work. First we begin by doing a special deep rhythmic breathing visualization. When inhaling, we visualize white light, the prana. While exhaling, we let the tired, old, negative thoughts about the past go. Then we do some physical movements to release tension, movements that will move and stretch the body. This is folowed by more breathing, but intended to quiet the patient, for this quiet breathing brings balance and harmony. We then go into silence together, and finally we say a prayer of gratitude for our lives. (You can make up your own prayer, but include the fact that you are excited and happy about being alive!)

Then I relax the patient's body by giving a light, soothing, gentle massage, concentrating over the heart area. We need to remember that the hand is an extension of the heart, that it is a source of healing magnetism, and a channel for the "light." Once the patient is calm, I use my crystal pendulum to check the chakras for blocks or congestion. Sometimes I run my hand over the chakras and feel for heat. You will have to choose the method that you like the best. I happen to like my pendulum because the patient can see its movement, and it serves as a visual guide, actually showing where the blocks are located in the body. This also helps develop trust and communication between the patient and myself.

Although I select the stones that I am to use in an intuitive fashion, I follow the guidance previously discussed regarding the chakras and my choice of color and stone. I wash the stones, dry them, and lay them on the body, beginning with the first chakra. I concentrate the stones in the areas needed, and finish by putting them on the face and the third eye (sixth chakra). Most people hold a great deal of tension in the jaws, cheeks and forehead—this is why I like to use the stones on the face.

It is important to wash the stones before *and after* a treatment because of their sensitive receptivity to vibrations! Sometimes I recommend that the patient bathe just before the treatment. I always request that the patient at least wash hands before the treatment, and I wash my hands as well, bringing clean hands to the healing process.

I leave the stones on the body for twenty to thirty minutes, depending on the reactions of the patient. Never leave anyone alone during a treatment—stay with the patient the whole time the stones are on the body, so you can observe all the physical reactions taking place. If a stone should fall off the body during this period, it may mean that the stone has completed its work and should not be put back. After you practice for a while, there will be no doubt in your mind as to what the stone wants to do. (See Plates 9-16 for illustrations of healing work.)

Some readers may wonder what side of the body I work with the most. Usually, the patients lie on their backs and I work on the front of the body. However, when I am doing a massage, or if someone complains of a lot of back pain, I will put the stones on the back. Some readers may intuitively feel that they want to work on the patient's back, for the energy may be more pronounced there. To do this, just visualize the chakras from the other side. Most people like it when I work on the front of the body, for then they can watch me work if they wish.

SOME PATIENT'S REACTIONS
TO HEALING

It is with profound amazement that I observe the various reactions of people who receive the healing stones. I would like to share some of these experiences with you, as they may help you learn how some people may respond when you begin to do things. As you begin to work with the stones, you may have people who react very differently—or they, too, may react as my patients did.

Sometimes it appears that the patient goes into a deep sleep. The patient doesn't remember anything about the session, but feels extremely relaxed when it is over. This usually means that the patient was nervous and unbalanced at the moment of treatment, and the stones actually put him to sleep in order to create a deep healing and rebalancing without any interference.

I put a crystal on a man's forehead (the third eye), and he relates the following experience: "It felt cold and heavy at first, and as I relaxed it grew warmer, and with my eyes closed I could see the crystal clearly. It seemed filled with light. From the center of the crystal, rainbow colored rays started pouring out and I was filled with joy."

A woman had a vision in which she was filled with blue light. She then saw an image of a flock of birds flying out from her third eye into the sky. A man experienced the crystal as a white spiraling light which moved into his body, filling it and then coming out from the third eye as streams of light.

Another woman had a vision of three monks who led her to a valley where they showed her sand paintings in which the symbols had very deep personal meaning to her life. A female patient went back to the time of her father's death and saw him lying in his coffin. She was experiencing a fear of death. Then she saw the entrance to a cave. It was dark, but she decided to go in. In the cave was a very large crystal, and she climbed on it, lying on the crystal feeling very good and safe. Then she saw a fire buring in a stove and her last image was a room in which the walls were closing in on her. She spoke to them and asked them to give her space.

A man saw an image of himself with his right hand open and his left hand tightly closed into a fist. He realized clearly at that moment that the emotional and receptive (or feminine-feeling) part of himself needed to open. Another man had a similar experience in which he felt his right side was very large, while his left side became very small. They were both in need of a more integrated and balanced self.

In one session, a woman started feeling a great deal of pain rising from her heart into her throat. As she let go of the pain, she went deeply into the earth. She felt as if she were in the womb of her mother—warm, engulfing and loving. Her mother died when she was very young, and for the first time, she felt the Earth as her Universal Mother.

I was very touched by the experience that a man had after I put the crystals on all his chakras. He had never been to any kind of a workshop before and was very self-protective and closed. However, after the treatment, he openly shared with the group, saying, "I saw my head as a block of ice. Very slowly, from the point where the crystal was, I felt my head slowly melting." He had tears in his eyes and I knew that a gate had opened in his life.

A woman saw herself in a pyramid, wrapped as a mummy, and she knew that she was believed to be dead. She, however, knew that she was not dead. Her left arm was covered by heavy stones that were very painful. She heard a voice saying, "All you have to do is to take away your arm." She became thirsty and wanted water. In her next image, she was in water, and she was having trouble breathing. Then she saw herself wrapped as a mummy again, but she had more space to move—her hands were able to move. Yet she felt a great heaviness in herself.

Another dramatic reaction occurred when I put a number of stones on a woman. She became very agitated and restless. It seemed that the stones were working on a deep level, trying to bring old emotions to the surface. Her hands started making very sharp and martial movements. She began to speak in an unknown and ancient language. She saw an image of herself, in a past life, as a warrior who had been sent out of the village after having lost a challenge. She felt that she had lost face, was dishonored and homeless. We were able, through this powerful experience, to touch on an old life pattern that had started then, and that had caused her great suffering in her present life.

Once I removed the stones from a man's heart and he felt the light go out. He experienced his heart as a black stone. He became aware at that moment that the darkness in his heart was the pain he had been carrying for many years regarding his father.

A woman, at the end of a treatment, looked up to me in a state of bliss and said, "You, too, are a stone—I love the stones. I feel my mother, the earth, protecting me and holding me. I can let go and relax knowing the earth is my home."

One woman said the stones felt very cold at first. As she relaxed, she felt and saw a warm energy rising from her feet, into her inner legs. It was a warm brown earth color. This energy rose up to her solar plexus, where she felt a great opening. She heard a voice and as she looked, she saw a large, brown stone between her feet, and it was speaking to her. First she thought, "This is impossible. Stones do not speak." But the stone continued, saying, "I am your friend, your ally. I will guide you and give you love." Then a great opening happened in her solar plexus. From there she felt a path to her heart. It was filled with light and she no longer felt any pain. She then saw a deep blue velvet cloth behind the stone, and a crystal on top of the stone. She cried from joy, knowing that the earth was her friend. She was later very much attracted to a carnelian and chose one as her stone.

Another woman had a vision of a crystal palace up on a hill. However, she had to go through a thick forest and climb very high before she could get to this palace. As she got closer, the crystal palace lit up as if waiting for her arrival. Then she saw herself in water and was able to float there.

. . .

All these visions and feelings give deep insight into areas of our lives. They are to be used to understand the blocks, the conflicts and difficulties that we all carry with us. Just like dreams, we can learn from the visions we experience during a stone healing treatment.

The crystals and stones work with the moment. The experiences are different each time. The stones work on very deep levels that we are unable to conceive. The purpose of the treatments is to open up and let out whatever is there, not to hold back, but to become aware. It is necessary to go with your feelings, to express emotions. Don't pretend they are not there. Help the people you work on to feel comfortable expressing themselves. Many will see their need to be more receptive. Some will be able to let go of the intellectual dialogue that has prevented them from getting in touch with their inner selves. Many of us carry memories in our subconscious, and these memories prevent us from truly living in the here and now. We can let that go.

Fear, hatred, jealousy, and all negative feelings initiate a chain of action and reaction according to the law of cause and effect. Whether the energy is a remnant of a past incarnation, or of this life cycle, the old energy of the remnant can haunt us like ghosts. Let it go.

All during the healing session I stay with the patient, soothing, calming, guiding, holding, counseling, doing whatever is needed. All patients, no matter what their unique experience has been, come out of the treatment feeling more calm and balanced, more open and receptive, in tune with themselves and with the cosmos. Through the crystals and stones they re-establish their connection with the earth, and they become more accepting of their place and purpose here on this wondrous planet.

The stones give us a message of beauty and love, of infinite compassion and harmony of light. As we open our hearts to the stones, to the soul inherent in all, our own soul will find peace. The radiance of eternal beauty shines throughout the universe, and the love that moves the stars can lead us to the light.

From the Tibetan Buddhist tradition comes this Sacred Mantra:

Om Mani Padme
Hum
(Jewel in the Lotus)

Let us all be the Jewels in the Lotus!

Prayer

O Mother Earth

My heart is full of Gratitude
For your divine gifts of
Abundance, Beauty and Love
May we be blessed to give back
By becoming Brilliant Jewels
Spreading with Humility
Knowledge, Service and Compassion
To Humanity.

Om

APPENDIX

Many readers may find the brief descriptions of the stones listed in this appendix an easy reference for both physical and spiritual symptoms. Table 1 lists the stones used for general healing, and includes a description of some of the imbalances that relate to them. Table 2 shows the stones in relation to the chakras. Readers should bear in mind that the color of each stone relates to one of the seven chakras, and when laying on the stones, the colors that apply to a particular chakra should only be used on that chakra.

Table 1. Stones Used for General Healing

Stone	Physical Cure	Spiritual Effect
Crystal	Balances and harmonizes the aura, giving equilbrium to the body. Decrystallizes congestions and blocks so energy can flow freely. Helps against dizziness, hemorrhage and diarrhea.	Helps our intuitive insight so we may become our own light.
Diamond	Offers great protection against negative thoughts and vibrations. A great help against poisoning.	Highest symbol of white light to help us toward transformation, to reach a state of non-duality so we can use this light in every aspect. of our being.
Moonstone	Great help to calm and soothe emotional reactions. Stimulates the pineal gland to assist in the growth process. Deals with mild endocrine imbalances in women. Can help clear congested lymphatics.	Bestows inner growth and strength. Opens us to the feminine feeling part of the personality, so we can integrate the entire self into oneness.
Opal	The different colors work on more than one center. The black opal works on all centers to equalize and balance.	Lifts ordinary consciousness to cosmic awareness. Helps us to reach highest spiritual levels of inner sight.
Pearl	Has high calcium content that contains currative properties for those who lack it.	Leads to purification through self-confrontation and a commitment to responsibility. Helps us reach a higher level through the practice of sacrifice and devotional love.
Black Tourmaline	Provides a protective shield against all negative energies. Most beneficial of all black stones.	Teaches us that life must have form to become a part of manifestation; helps with dreams and abstract thoughts by making them more real.

Table 1 continued.

Stone	Physical Cure	Spiritual Effect
Smoky Quartz	Much like Black Tourmaline. Provides a shield of protection. Was worn by ancient priests and priestessess in the mystery temples. Symbolizes the deeper truths.	Teaches us light within the darkness. Aids our inner search so we can integrate and transform our shadows in light.

Table 2. Using the Stones in Relation to the Chakra

THE FIRST CHAKRA

Stone	Physical Cure	Spiritual Effect
Ruby	Activates and vitalizes the body through the action of the blood stream. Used also to prevent miscarriages.	Lifts the heart toward selflessness and compassion for all human beings.
Coral	Creates a heating influence on the body. Aids in anemia, deficient nutrition, lethargy. Good for women in times of menstruation Can be used against colic.	Teaches form and flexibility.
Garnet	Stimulates the sex drive. Aids the generative system. Good against depression, rheumatism and arthritis.	Raises the spirit from passion to purity.
Red Jasper	Provides earth energy for protection. Aids liver, stomach troubles, and infections.	Bestows the strength of the earth.
Bloodstone	Invigorates and stimulates the whole being. Aids in bladder problems.	Helps us to trust in life and to understand the warmth of the earth.

THE SECOND CHAKRA

Stone	Physical Cure	Spiritual Effect
Carnelian	For grounding and anchoring. Influences and regulates food intake and assimilation. Helps against blood poisoning, rheumatism and wounds.	Instills feelings of wellbeing and belonging on earth. Also indicates inflowing power.
Fire Opal	Breaks up all forms of crystallization. Aids the digestive system. Gives an energy boost when needed.	Helps us link to higher self, creating less separation. Restores suppressed feelings.

Table 2 continued.

THE THIRD CHAKRA

Stone	Physical Cure	Spiritual Effect
Topaz Gold	Helps focus thoughts. Gives strength to heart. Balances nervous system and solar plexus. Affects the spinal column. Promotes mental and physical digestion. Good against coldness—restores the sense of taste (from the liver).	Inspiring and stimulating influence on higher mind and soul. Helps self to become more aware. Helps soul in its determination to reach enlightenment.
Amber	Purifies and cleans the system. Helps the digestive system and endocrine glands. Gives warmth. For adults: aids solar plexus, liver, asthma, and infection. For babies: helps the teething process.	Strength, wisdom and peace.
Citrine Quartz	Lighter shades are of great benefit to endocrine glands. Cleansing and purifying influence. Darker shades work on removing fears which block solar plexus. Helps diabetes. Purifies and cleans the skin. Strong against depression.	Stimulates cosmic consciousness. Lifts the soul toward understanding and compassion.

THE FOURTH CHAKRA

Stone	Physical Cure	Spiritual Effect
Tourmaline (in general)	Unsurpassed aid for nervous system. Maintains balance on all levels.	For using the different shades of color follow the color Chakras.
Rubellite (Pink Tourmaline)	Subtly balances the heart center. Increases depth of insight and preception.	Teaches us to lead from the heart. Strengthens the will to love and sacrifice. Opens the heart to self-devotional urges.

Table 2 continued.

Stone	Physical Cure	Spiritual Effect
Water-mellon Tourmaline	Balances polarity. Healing and harmonizing influence on heart and nervous system. Aids in altering cellular structure. Helps to prevent cancer because of continuous balancing emanations, preventing irregular cell growth. Good protection to wear.	Teaches us to be self-contained, integrated, secure in ourselves. Helps us become more open and flexible. Allows us to use the heart chakra more fully.
Kunzite	Removes and alleviates the heart from old pain and suffering. Brings softness, light, and truth to the heart.	Links the heart emotions to the higher realms so the individual will be able to experience the infinite love of the spirit.
Rhodochrosite	Integrates the physical, mental, and emotional triad. Is good conductor of energy. Warm, soothes the heart. Beneficient to the wearer.	Increases creative thinking process. Instills love of life.
Emerald	Aids in developing a revitalized, beautiful physical body. Balances and heals. Gives peace to body and heart. Normalizes blood pressure. Good for eye infections.	New birth. Provides a serene inner lift—abundance and richness. Potential to reveal the mysteries of heaven and earth. Helps self-control and maturity.
Malachite	Heals and balances the whole system. Aids functions of pancreas and spleen. Good for eye infections, asthma, menstrual disorders, poisoning and rheumatism.	Teaches that through the process of creation we understand spirit. Reveals our deepest fears about change and growth. Mirrors the soul.
Jade	Calming and quieting. Overall healing and balancing influence. Good for childbirth, influenza, neuralgia, migraine.	Giver of virtues: humility, wisdom, justice, courage. Consciousness raising.
Green Tourmaline	Quiets the mind via the nervous system. Potential for regenerating and rejuvenating entire body. Good for inflammation, asthma, heart, influenza, cancer. Normalizes blood pressure.	Creates the will to achieve wisdom and to ease conflicts. Realigns the mental body by shattering old concepts and pushing us to begin anew on a different level of consciousness.

Table 2 continued.

Stone	Physical Cure	Spiritual Effect
Green and Colorless Tourmaline	Calms and balances the brain and nerve fluids. Potentila for reducing inflammations, headaches, and epileptic seizures.	Like green tourmaline, it adds light to enhance clarity of purpose.
Chrysoprase	Sedative and tranquilizing effect like jade. Creates balance and purpose to all with neurotic patterns of behavior. Good for the heart, bleeding, hemorrhage, childbirth. Influences the glands.	Clarifies problems bringing unconscious thoughts to consciousness and strengthening inner vision.
Peridot	Calming, purifying and balancing for the physical body. Has cleansing effects. Good for digestion of foods; relieves constipation; helps inflamed conditions of the bowel. Relieves melancholia.	Helps to develop mental capabilities, supplies balance and tranquility to emotions. Opens the inner sight to the spiritual sun.

THE FIFTH CHAKRA

Stone	Physical Cure	Spiritual Effect
Aquamarine	Excellent purifier for throat congestion. Balances and stabilizes the body; helps against nerve pains, gland troubles, disorders of neck, jaw, throat, teeth. Great filter.	Bestows purity and innocence. Clarity of vision. Sensitive understanding.
Turquoise	Strong healing vibrations magnified by high copper content. Good for heart, chest, neck, lungs, respiratory system, also for eyes.	Teaches infinity of sea and sky, purity of spirit.

Table 2 continued.

Stone	Physical Cure	Spiritual Effect
Chrysocolla	Balances and calms the heart and emotions. Alleviates fears bringing peace to heart. Helps prevent ulcers and digestive tract difficulties.	Resembles turquoise but moves us into a higher consciousness. More balance and harmony for emotions and heart.
Sapphire (Blue)	Very healing on throat center. Purification. Lowers blood pressure. Soothes pain, cools fevers, good against nervousness, insomnia.	Potential to transform and lift the soul into higher realms. Inspires devotion, meditation, and truth.
Lapis Lazuli	Healing throat congestion; great aid in swellings, stings, inflammations, rashes. Good against depression and nervous headaches, helps fevers and high blood pressure, and painful menstruation.	Instills high idealism, fellowship and cooperation. Inspires our eternal soul to understand immortality.
Topaz (Blue)	Cooling, calming, purifying to nerves or throat. Strong electrical and magnetic power. Good for nervous headaches, palpitations.	Intensifies creative energy flow by giving inspiration to artists of any type

THE SIXTH CHAKRA		
Stone	Physical Cure	Spiritual Effect
Indigo Sapphire	Great healing value in treatment of mental disorders, delirium, melancholy, all derangements of the thinking capacity. Good against insomnia. Strengthens and heals sense organs.	Potential to develop our intuitive and clairvoyant perception so we may see truth and reach wisdom.
Azurite	A great healer in any area of the body as it vitalizes parts that have been damaged. Helps mind to retain information.	Opens us to inner sight, to perceptions of the ultimate truth and cosmic awareness. Bestows consciousness and a sense of duty.

Table 2 continued.

THE SEVENTH CHAKRA

Stone	Physical Cure	Spiritual Effect
Amethyst	High density vibration which is potent for all forms of pain. Dispells anger, rage, fear, anxiety. Brings comfort and relief to the psychologically ill. Good for treating impurities of blood and in venereal diseases. Great aid in headaches, migraines, insomnia. Balances and stabilizes problems of sexual polarity. Good against color-blindness and problems with alcohol.	Transmutation — inspires and encourages meditation, selfless giving, and service to humanity.
Fluorite	In shades of violet, it is much like the amethyst. In shades of green, it aids the individual in his ability to handle many high frequency vibrations, thus calming the nervous system.	Leads to inspirational devotion, cosmic truths and wisdom.

INDEX

Numbers in italics refer to the complete discussion of the stone.